Lectionary Worship Aids

REVISED FOR USE
WITH THE
COMMON (CONSENSUS)
LECTIONARY

SERIES B

HETH H. CORL

C.S.S. Publishing Company
Lima, Ohio

LECTIONARY WORSHIP AIDS SERIES B

Copyright © 1984 by
The C.S.S. Publishing Company, Inc.
Lima, Ohio

All rights reserved: No portion of this book may be reproduced or utilized in any form or by any means, electronic or mechanical including photocopying, without permission in writing from the publisher. Inquiries should be addressed to: The C.S.S. Publishing Company, Inc., 628 South Main Street, Lima, Ohio 45804

4868/ISBN 0-89536-690-8　　　　　　　　　　　　　PRINTED IN U.S.A.

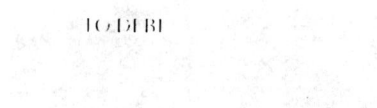

TABLE OF CONTENTS

Publisher's Preface................................... vii
Foreword... viii
Introduction.. ix

Advent-Christmas Season
    First Sunday in Advent........................... 1
    Second Sunday in Advent......................... 4
    Third Sunday in Advent.......................... 7
    Fourth Sunday in Advent......................... 10
    Christmas, First Proper.......................... 13
    Christmas, Second Proper........................ 16
    Christmas, Third Proper......................... 19
    First Sunday After Christmas..................... 22
    Second Sunday After Christmas................... 28
    The Epiphany.................................... 31

Season after the Epiphany
    First Sunday After the Epiphany.................. 34
    Second Sunday After the Epiphany................ 37
    Third Sunday After the Epiphany................. 40
    Fourth Sunday After the Epiphany................ 43
    Fifth Sunday After the Epiphany.................. 46
    Sixth Sunday After the Epiphany.................. 49
    Seventh Sunday After the Epiphany............... 52
    Eighth Sunday After the Epiphany................ 55
    Last Sunday After the Epiphany.................. 58

Lenten Season
    Ash Wednesday.................................. 61
    First Sunday of Lent............................. 64
    Second Sunday of Lent........................... 67
    Third Sunday of Lent............................ 70
    Fourth Sunday of Lent........................... 73
    Fifth Sunday of Lent............................. 76
    Sixth Sunday of Lent (Passion Sunday)............ 79
    Sixth Sunday of Lent (Palm Sunday).............. 82
    Monday in Holy Week............................ 85
    Tuesday in Holy Week........................... 88
    Wednesday in Holy Week........................ 91
    Thursday in Holy Week.......................... 94
    Good Friday..................................... 97

Easter Season
   Easter Day 100
   Second Sunday of Easter 103
   Third Sunday of Easter 106
   Fourth Sunday of Easter 109
   Fifth Sunday of Easter 112
   Sixth Sunday of Easter 115
   Ascension 118
   Seventh Sunday of Easter 121

Season of Pentecost
   The Day of Pentecost 124
   First Sunday After Pentecost (Trinity Sunday) . 127
   Proper 4 130
   Proper 5 133
   Proper 6 136
   Proper 7 139
   Proper 8 142
   Proper 9 145
   Proper 10 148
   Proper 11 151
   Proper 12 154
   Proper 13 157
   Proper 14 160
   Proper 15 163
   Proper 16 166
   Proper 17 169
   Proper 18 172
   Proper 19 175
   Proper 20 178
   Proper 21 181
   Proper 22 184
   Proper 23 187
   Proper 24 190
   Proper 25 193
   Proper 26 196
   Proper 27 199
   Proper 28 202
   Proper 29 205

All Saints' Day 208
Thanksgiving Day 211
Topical Index 215
Index of Scriptures 219

PUBLISHER'S PREFACE

The worship elements provided in **Lectionary Worship Aids — Series B** are offered by the C.S.S. Publishing Company as resources to enrich the worship experience for those who utilize them.

Although this volume is copyrighted, the publishers will permit the printing or mimeographing of any elements contained herein, when the printing or mimeographing is for use during a worship service. All other reproduction is, of course, protected by the copyright.

We hope that your use of these materials will prove beneficial in your worship.

The C.S.S. Publishing Company

Foreword

The increasing use during the past fifteen years of the various denominational versions of the three-year ecumenical lectionary has now resulted in a second generation ecumenical lectionary. The Common Lectionary, as it is called, reduces to a minimum the denominational variations in the lectionary and responds to criticisms of the lectionary that have been received, especially its use of the Old Testament.

One of the advantages of the three-year lectionary has been the wealth of worship and preaching resources which it has stimulated. Creative ministers have not only been helped to plan their own congregation's worship, they have also been able to publish what they have done, so that other ministers might benefit from their creativity.

Heth Corl is a fine example of such a creative minister. His LECTIONARY WORSHIP AIDS has been a useful resource ever since it was first published, and now in revised form it will be more helpful than ever. The three sets of resources for every Sunday not only give the minister a wide range of choice for Sunday morning, they also provide resources for the church that has additional services Sunday evening or midweek.

It is my hope that ministers using these resources will be free and creative enough to choose what best fits the realities of their local situations, to make adaptations, and to be prompted by these examples to develop their own ideas and acts of worship. Perhaps out of this collection will come resources written by others that can be, in turn, published and shared. Through this process of sharing, ministers and congregations who wish vital and creative worship stand greatly to benefit.

Hoyt L. Hickman
Section on Worship
Board of Discipleship
The United Methodist Church

INTRODUCTION

This new set of LECTIONARY WORSHIP AIDS has been revised to correspond with the Consensus Lectionary. The three year lectionary prepared by the Consultation on Church Union in 1974 became widely used throughout many denominations. However, there were some problems inherent, so that to make the lectionary as ecumenical as the denominations using it, a revision was necessary. Variations in the dating system for the Sundays after Pentecost had not been dealt with in the lectionary. The Old Testament lessons had been chosen primarily to correspond with the Gospel, limiting the message of the Old Testament. Verses within the lections varied from a few to many.

Consequently, the Consultation on Common Texts created the North American Committee on Calendar and Lectionary in 1978, to develop a consensus lectionary. It is this lectionary for which *Lectionary Worship Aids* has been revised.

The Gospel lessons have remained basically unchanged. The greatest changes have been made in the Old Testament lessons. Many of the lections have been changed only by the specific verses selected. New Year's Day and Thanksgiving have been added to the lectionary, as have additional readings for Christmas Eve/Day. There is now agreement on dating the Sundays after Pentecost.

Whether or not your congregation follows the lectionary, these worship resources can be helpful in preparing a worship service. All Scriptures used in these resources have been indexed. Begin with the Scripture you have selected for a particular service. If that Scripture is listed in the index of Scriptures, it will refer to resources based on that text which may be appropriate, even though that text has been selected for a different Sunday of the Christian Year. The same thing can be done with the Topical Index.

These resources provide continuity in the service of worship by following the theme derived from the lesson selected for the day. Each lection has three lessons: the First Lesson, an Old Testament reading except when Acts is read during the Easter Season; the Second Lesson, one of the New Testament books other than the Gospels; and the Gospel. A set of resources is provided for each of the three lessons, even though only one will be used for a given service. Thus for each service, a pastor may choose to read all three lessons from the lection, but use only the resources for the lesson from which he or she chooses a text for the sermon.

The resources are also biblical. They are based on Scripture, but are not quotations of Scripture. A variety of translations and commentaries was used in an exegetical study to develop resources that would be true to the Scripture being read and interpreted in the act of worship.

The resources are of a length which permits them to be mimeographed in a regular size bulletin using elite type. A worship service using the Call to Worship, Collect, and Prayer of Confession can be typed on the inside pages in the order of service, allowing the back page to be used for concerns of the congregation.

Each church is accustomed to its own order of service. The use of these resources does not need to change that order. However, they have been written from a point of view which interprets the act of worship through this general outline: God calls us to worship him. We respond with praise and thanksgiving. God speaks to us through his Word. Hearing that Word, we confess our sins. Assured of our forgiveness, we give ourselves in dedication. We then intercede on behalf of others. The order concludes with God's departing blessing. This order places the Prayer of Confession after the sermon which lifts up a particular area in which we need to examine ourselves. We then confess our failure in that area, followed by a dedication of ourselves in discipleship in that particular area. An order which places the Prayer of Confession earlier in the service would not limit the use of these resources.

I am grateful to Hoyt L. Hickman, Edwin E. Burtner, and James F. White, all of whom gave valuable advice in the development and writing of these worship aids. I am also indebted to my wife, Karen, for typing the manuscript.

It is my hope that these aids to worship will assist congregations in expressing their worship of God with words which speak on their behalf in ways that are true to their faith.

— Heth H. Corl

FIRST SUNDAY IN ADVENT

First Lesson: Isaiah 63:16 — 64:8
Theme: A plea for God to come in mercy

Call to Worship

Pastor: We are people with a Christian heritage. But much of our Christianity is missing its Christ.

People: Out of the depths of our sinfulness, we cry to God to come to us in his great mercy.

Pastor: He is our God, and we are his children. He will hear our cry and come to us.

People: We yield ourselves to God as clay in the potter's hand, confident he will remold us through Christ Jesus his Son.

Collect

Merciful Father, who sees through our insincere expressions of faith; and who has sent your only Son to bring healing and restoration: Come to us in the advent of your Son, that we may surrender our artificial forms of faith, and come alive in Christ our Savior, through whom we pray. Amen.

Prayer of Confession

Father, we are sick with sin, and unhappy in our misery. But many of us do not care, or cannot find the will to change. Forgive us for pretending with our faith by not letting it be the foundation on which we build our lives. Cause us to see the tragedy of our situation; that we may eagerly look for the advent of your Son to bring us the gift of your mercy and new life. In his name we pray. Amen.

Hymns

"Come, Thou Long-Expected Jesus"
"Have Thine Own Way, Lord"
"O Come, O Come, Emmanuel"
"Out of the Depths I Cry to Thee"

FIRST SUNDAY IN ADVENT

Second Lesson: 1 Corinthians 1:3-9
Theme: Waiting for Christ to be revealed.

Call to Worship
Pastor: Let us thank God for the grace he has given us through Jesus Christ.
People: God has blessed us with many gifts in our Christian experience.
Pastor: Rich as God has made us in our faith, we still look expectantly for a fuller revelation of Christ.
People: May God keep us firm in our faith, so that we will be prepared for Christ's return.

Collect
Almighty God, who has blessed us abundantly with spiritual gifts: Keep us in union with Christ our Lord; that we may be firmly established in our faith, fully prepared for the Day when we shall see our Lord face to face. In his name we pray. Amen.

Prayer of Confession
We confess, Father, that there are times when we are possessive and proud of the spiritual gifts with which you have blessed us. And yet our Christian experience is so immature compared with Christ's glory yet to be revealed. Forgive us when we glory in our gifts rather than wait expectantly for Christ's glory to be further revealed. Help us prepare ourselves to be faithful disciples until his Day becomes our blessing. In our Savior's name we pray. Amen.

Hymns
"Come, Thou Almighty King"
"Lo, He Comes with Clouds Descending"
"The King Shall Come"
"Watchmen, Tell Us of the Night"

FIRST SUNDAY IN ADVENT

Gospel: Mark 13:32-37
Theme: Be alert for Christ's return

Call to Worship

Leader: ~~Pastor:~~ We know Christ has come. But we know also that there is a future tense to his advent.

People: **We know what joy his first advent brought to the world. But we give little thought to his return.**

Leader: ~~Pastor:~~ Jesus said to stay awake. That is, live in readiness for his return, because we do not know when it will be.

People: **May our lives witness to hearts which are open and ready for him at any time!**

Collect

Gracious Father, whose Son brought joy to our world in his first advent: Help us to be alert in our discipleship, that we may be ready to share in the joy of his return whenever it may be. In his name we pray. Amen.

Prayer of Confession

For generations, Father, Christians have talked about Jesus' return. And the repetitious call to readiness has made us indifferent to being prepared. Forgive us for the absence of expectancy in our hearts, and uncommitted discipleship in our living. We simply are not ready for such a glorious event. Stir us with great expectations, that we may live as Christians prepared for our Lord to come. In his name we pray. Amen.

Hymns

"I Know Not What the Future Hath"
"Lord Christ, When First Thou Cam'st"
"My Soul, Be on Thy Guard"
"Wake, Awake, for Night Is Flying"

SECOND SUNDAY IN ADVENT

First Lesson: Isaiah 40:1-11
Theme: Prepare the way for God to come to us

Call to Worship

Pastor: When God promises comfort to his people, we can be sure something wonderful will happen!

People: Christ's advent is indeed our source of God's comfort which he has proclaimed to his people.

Pastor: With God's promise of comfort comes his order to prepare our hearts for a new life, disciplined with devotion, and blessed with his presence.

People: May every heart make preparation for God to lead us to his Son, that we may enjoy his salvation.

Collect

Almighty God, who speaks through your messengers, calling us to prepare our lives for your advent: Cause us to hear that voice, that we may make ready our lives for you to lead us into the joy and comfort which is found in Christ Jesus your Son, in whose name we pray. Amen.

Prayer of Confession

O God, we want life to be full of joy, peace, and comfort. But we yield to the rough and crooked ways of life instead of disciplining ourselves in preparation for you to lead us in the blessing of your comfort. Forgive us for our constant sinning which prevents you from coming to us. Stir our hearts to see your glory revealed in the advent of your Son, that we may submit to his rule and authority in our lives. In his name we pray. Amen.

Hymns

"Guide Me, O Thou Great Jehovah"
"Lead, Kindly Light"
"O Come, and Dwell in Me"
"There's a Voice in the Wilderness Crying"

SECOND SUNDAY IN ADVENT

Second Lesson: 2 Peter 3:8-15a
Theme: Be holy and dedicated to God

Call to Worship

Pastor: God calls us to righteous living in preparation for the new heaven and earth he has promised.

People: We hear God's call, and know he wants us to turn away from our sins.

Pastor: God's peace is ours when we do our best to be holy and dedicated to him.

People: We thank God for his patience with us, and his willingness to help us live in righteousness.

Collect

Gracious Father, whose judgment on our sins is delayed by your patience with our sinfulness: Inspire us to turn from our sins to live holy lives; that we may be found faultless in judgment through the grace of our Lord Jesus Christ, whose advent is the hope of the world. In his name we pray. Amen.

Prayer of Confession

We wonder, Father, as sinful as the human race is, will the world ever come to an end? For you are so patient and so willing to wait for us to turn from sin before the final advent of Christ. Forgive us for our unholy lives which delay the glory you are waiting to share with us. Give us a desire to live dedicated lives, that we may be prepared to be citizens in your glorious kingdom. We pray through Christ our Lord. Amen.

Hymns

"Blest Are the Pure in Heart"
"Lift Up Your Heads, Ye Mighty Gates"
"Love Divine, All Loves Excelling"
"Take Time to Be Holy"

SECOND SUNDAY IN ADVENT

Gospel: Mark 1:1-8
Theme: Turn from your sins

Call to Worship

Leader: Christ has come, but if he is to come into our lives, we must prepare the way for him.

People: **If Christ's advent is to others only, that does not bring joy to us. We want to prepare for his advent to us.**

Leader: When we turn from our sins and make room in our lives for Christ, he comes, just as surely as Christmas!

People: **Thank God for his call to repentance! May he enable us to turn from sin to accept his Son.**

Collect

Most merciful Father, who calls us to turn from our sins in preparation to receive your Son as Lord and Savior: Accept our confessions as we open our hearts to Jesus, that his advent may fill our lives with your Spirit. In his name we pray. Amen.

Prayer of Confession

We hear that voice in the wilderness, Father, urging us to change our ways by turning from sin. And so we come to you, confessing that we are sinners who want to be forgiven. Forgive us for all that keeps Christ from coming into our lives with full control. Let his advent be a gift of new life in which we are led by your Spirit in true devotion. In Christ's name we pray. Amen.

Hymns

"Come, Every Soul by Sin Oppressed"
"Jesus Is Tenderly Calling"
"Just as I Am, without One Plea"
"There's a Voice in the Wilderness Crying"

THIRD SUNDAY IN ADVENT

First Lesson: Isaiah 61:1-4, 8-11
Theme: Good news of the Messiah's mission

Call to Worship

Pastor: Listen! We have good news from God our Father!
People: We are filled with joy in anticipation of what God has promised to do through his Son.
Pastor: God has sent his Son with a ministry of deliverance, forgiveness, and hope.
People: Hail to the Lord's anointed! He comes to restore our lives with his saving grace!

Collect

Gracious Father, whose good tidings fill us with joy and gladness: Fulfill your message of peace and salvation in the advent of your Son Jesus; that our anticipation of joy may become a reality as we commit our lives in discipleship to him, our Lord and Savior, in whose name we pray. Amen.

Prayer of Confession

Father, we know the pain of sorrow, affliction, and oppression; not so much from outside forces, as from within. We take our lives out of your control, only to become less than whole persons. Forgive us for our disobedience and incompetent behavior. Come with your favor, and restore us to wholeness through your Son Jesus, our Savior, in whose name we pray. Amen.

Hymns

"Come, Thou Long-Expected Jesus"
"Hail to the Lord's Anointed"
"Of the Father's Love Begotten"
"Thou Hidden Source of Calm Repose"

THIRD SUNDAY IN ADVENT

Second Lesson: 1 Thessalonians 5:16-24
Theme: God keeps us faultless for Christ's return

Call to Worship

Pastor: The Christian life is filled with joy because God blesses us with his love.

People: We are thankful for each day, because God comes to us with new blessings, adding to our joy.

Pastor: God blesses our whole being, enabling us to be faithful to the righteous life, in preparation for Christ's return.

People: God is faithful to us with his love. May we be faithful to him with our lives, in thankful expectation for our Lord's coming.

Collect

Eternal God, who enables your children to live as disciples of Christ in expectation of his return: Keep our whole being, body, mind, and soul, free from the power of sin; that we may be ready for the coming of our Lord Jesus, in whose name we pray. Amen.

Prayer of Confession

We divide life into categories, Father, as though there were a righteous side of life and another side which is unaffected by our faith. Forgive us when we do not surrender our whole being to the guiding influence of your Holy Spirit. Fill our lives with joy through a total commitment of our being; that we may belong, without reservation, to Christ when he returns. In his name we pray. Amen.

Hymns

"I Want a Principle Within"
"Lo, He Comes with Clouds Descending"
"Rejoice, Rejoice, Believers"
"Take My Life, and Let It Be Consecrated"

THIRD SUNDAY IN ADVENT

Gospel: John 1:6-8, 19-28
Theme: Pointing the way to Christ

Call to Worship

Leader: God prepared the way for Jesus by sending John the Baptizer to preach repentance.
People: Important as John was, he was not the Messiah whom God had promised.
Leader: His ministry was much like the ministry of the church today. We are to point to Christ, not the church, as our source of salvation.
People: We want to be faithful to our mission, that we may be used of God to lead people through the church to Christ.

Collect

Gracious Father, who prepared the way for your Son with the message of John the Baptizer: Use your church today as your messenger, that our Lord may find penitent hearts and willing followers when he comes. In his name we pray. Amen.

Prayer of Confession

We know the church is yours, Father, to give you honor and glory through people who have turned from sin to live as your children. But we sometimes lose the vision of our purpose and redesign the church as an end in itself. Forgive us when we let your church get in the way of pointing others to Christ. Use us as messengers who will lift up Christ as our only hope of redemption, that we may prepare our world for his coming. In his name we pray. Amen.

Hymns

"Heralds of Christ"
"Lord, Speak to Me"
"There's a Voice in the Wilderness Crying"
"Watchman, Tell Us of the Night"

FOURTH SUNDAY IN ADVENT

First Lesson: 2 Samuel 7:8-16
Theme: Jesus is our hope

Call to Worship

Pastor: Our relationship with God gives us hope in situations when we feel hopeless.

People: We are full of hope because we believe God fulfills his promises through his Son, Jesus, our Savior.

Pastor: Jesus is the hope of our world. That is why his advent is a season of expectation and excitement.

People: We are eager to experience God's love fulfilled in the lives of all people through his Son, Jesus, our Savior!

Collect

Most merciful Father, who keeps hope alive in us because of the advent of your Son: Sustain us in our pilgrimage through life, blessed by the coming of Christ into our lives, that we may rejoice in the hope he gives to those who put their trust in him. In his name we pray. Amen.

Prayer of Confession

Father, we try so hard to build up your church with programs and projects, so it will be a strong institution in our society. We forget that it is you who are at work building us up to be strong in your kingdom by giving us hope through your Son. Forgive us when our hope is dimmed by indifference to the promised joy fulfilled in the advent of your Son. Renew our hope; that we may put our trust in Christ our Redeemer, in whose name we pray. Amen.

Hymns

"Come, Thou Long-Expected Jesus"
"Hope of the World"
"My Hope Is Built"
"The People That in Darkness Sat"

FOURTH SUNDAY IN ADVENT

Second Lesson: Romans 16:25-27
Theme: Praise to God for his revelation in Christ

Call to Worship

Pastor: The truth of God's salvation, written by the prophets of old, is revealed in Jesus Christ, God's Son.

People: We praise God for revealing his love to us in Jesus, our Savior, whose advent we celebrate.

Pastor: Many generations lived in expectation, waiting for God to act in a special way. We are blessed with knowing and experiencing that hope fulfilled.

People: We thank God for our salvation revealed in Jesus Christ, fulfilling the hope and expectation of many generations.

Collect

Eternal God, whose truth proclaimed by prophets of old has been revealed in the advent of your Son: Make us firm in our faith as strong disciples, that we may live in obedience to the truth you have revealed to us. We pray in our Savior's name. Amen.

Prayer of Confession

The message of your prophets means much more to us, Father, with the advent of Christ revealing your truth more clearly. Even then, we limit our response by not letting Christ come into our lives with salvation. Forgive us when we turn our backs on the truth revealed in Jesus. Turn us around in eager acceptance of your Son, that your revelation in Christ may become the story of our salvation. In his name we pray. Amen.

Hymns

"Good Christian Men, Rejoice"
"Joy to the Word"
"Rejoice, the Lord Is King"
"Thanks to God Whose Word Was Spoken"

FOURTH SUNDAY IN ADVENT

Gospel: Luke 1:26-38
Theme: Jesus' divine origin

Call to Worship

Pastor: God's Word became flesh, not by the act of man, but by the creative act of the Holy Spirit.
People: We believe Jesus' divine origin is God's way of making salvation available to all sinners.
Pastor: Redemption is not ours to create or control. It is God's love, God's initiative, God's act. And it comes to us through his Son.
People: We celebrate, with joy and thanksgiving, the birth of God's Son, our divine Lord and Savior!

Collect

O God of love and redemption, who delivers salvation to us through the beautiful experience of your Son's birth: Draw us to him in adoration and devotion, that the redemption he imparts may have effect in our lives. In his name we pray. Amen.

Prayer of Confession

We love the baby in the manger, Father, but such adoration does not necessarily express true devotion to your Son who came to be our Savior. Forgive us for sentimental rituals which dramatize an unwanted baby while our lives continue to dramatize an unwanted Savior. Lead us to a salvation experience at the manger; that we may celebrate the Christ event in Jesus' birth. In his name we pray. Amen.

Hymns

"Gentle Mary Laid Her Child"
"O Come, O Come, Emmanuel"
"O Son of God Incarnate"
"What Child Is This"

CHRISTMAS, FIRST PROPER
(Christmas Eve/Day)

First Lesson: Isaiah 9:2-7
Theme: For those in darkness, a gift of joy

Call to Worship

Pastor: We have good news for those who live in the shadows of life!
People: God has poured out the brightness of his love, that we may be filled with joy!
Pastor: Because Jesus was born, we have joy that knows no bounds.
People: We rejoice in what God has done, turning our darkness of sin into the brilliance of his glory.

Collect

Father in heaven, whose glorious love dissolves our sin as light dispels darkness: Shine into our hearts with your redeeming love; that we may have the joy of Christ's birth blessing us deep within our hearts. We pray in Jesus' name. Amen.

Prayer of Confession

We know why darkness symbolizes life without you, Father. Too often we try to find our own way, rejecting the light with which you would direct us. Forgive us for independence that drives us further into darkness, cheating us of the joy you offer in Christ. Give us the experience of your light flooding our souls with the joy of living with, and for, and like our Savior, in whose name we pray. Amen.

Hymns

"All My Heart This Night Rejoices"
"God Rest You Merry Gentlemen"
"Good Christian Men, Rejoice"
"Joy to the World"

CHRISTMAS, FIRST PROPER
(Christmas Eve/Day)

Second Lesson: Titus 2:11-14
Theme: God's salvation, a gift of grace

Call to Worship

Pastor: God has revealed his grace in the birth of his Son.
People: We rejoice in the grace of God that saves us from sin.
Pastor: May the birth of Christ inspire us to accept the grace God offers, and live our lives to his honor and glory.
People: We are eager to give ourselves to God in thanksgiving for the gift of his Son.

Collect

Gracious Father, who calls us by your grace to live our lives holy unto you: Grant us your Spirit; that we may have the desire and the strength to surrender to you the control of our lives. In the name of Christ we pray. Amen.

Prayer of Confession

Father in heaven, we confess that our lives contradict what our lips say about our allegiance. Forgive us when we live in disobedience to your will. Cleanse us, and make us yours, eager to follow your will. We pray in our Savior's name. Amen

Hymns

"Away in a Manger"
"O Little Town of Bethlehem"
"Silent Night, Holy Night"
"What Child Is This"

CHRISTMAS, FIRST PROPER
(Christmas Eve/Day)

Gospel: Luke 2:1-20
Theme: The birth of Christ, a gift of peace

Call to Worship
Pastor: Come, all you who are faithful, and worship the Christ Child, whose birth we celebrate.
People: We come to worship our Savior, Christ the Lord.
Pastor: Glory to God in the highest!
People: Peace to all with whom God is pleased!

Collect
Most gracious Father, whose gift of peace became incarnate in your Son: Bless us this holy season with the assurance that your peace is indeed a reality for us; that as we celebrate our Savior's birth we may be motivated to share that peace with our world. In our Savior's name we pray. Amen.

Prayer of Confession
Every year we celebrate our Savior's birth, Father, yet every year we need to affirm once again the gift of peace expressed in his birth. Forgive us when our behavior denies that peace, contradicting the faith we now profess. Come into our hearts with your transforming power that will ward off all threats to our being peacemakers in our Lord's service. In his name we pray. Amen.

Hymns
"Hark! The Herald Angels Sing"
"It Came Upon the Midnight Clear"
"O Come, All Ye Faithful"
"The First Noel"

CHRISTMAS, SECOND PROPER
(Additional Lessons for Christmas Day)

First Lesson: Isaiah 62:6-7, 10-12
Theme: The Lord announces salvation

Call to Worship

Pastor: Rejoice! God's salvation has come to us in the birth of his Son!

People: Glory to God our Father! He has seen us in our sin, yet claims us as his children!

Pastor: We who are sinners can now be called Christians; because Christ is born, a Savior of sinners.

People: We come to God who has come to us, bound together in reconciliation by the birth of Jesus, his Son!

Collect

Almighty God, our heavenly Father, whose Son was born to rescue us from sin: Give us a new name as you reclaim us, that our world may know Christ has come to give salvation to all people. In his name we pray. Amen.

Prayer of Confession

It is hard for us to understand what has happened, Father. You have changed our name, and we are called Christian. But we are more familiar with our old name, sinner. Forgive us when we celebrate your entrance into our world, without becoming the new being your salvation brings. As we celebrate Christ's birth, help us to become Christ-bearers, that our world may know none are forsaken. We pray through Christ our Lord. Amen.

Hymns

"Good Christian Men, Rejoice"
"I Know Not How That Bethlehem's Babe"
"Love Came Down at Christmas"
"There's a Song in the Air"

CHRISTMAS, SECOND PROPER
(Additional Lessons for Christmas Day)

Second Lesson: Titus 3:4-7
Theme: Saved to new life by Jesus

Call to Worship

Pastor: God has revealed his love to us through his Son, and desires to save us from sin.
People: Salvation has come to us in Jesus, whose birth we celebrate with joy.
Pastor: The joy of Christmas is the new life we are able to live, having been rescued from a life of sin.
**People: We celebrate with joy:
God's love for us;
His Son who came to be our Savior; and
The new life to which we have been saved!**

Collect

Most gracious Father, whose redeeming love cleanses us from sin to live a new life with Christ: Let our Lord's birth be the instrument through which your Holy Spirit may reach us, that we may be washed clean to dwell with you forever. We pray through Christ our Lord. Amen.

Prayer of Confession

Happiness has reached its peak, our Father, as we celebrate our Savior's birth. Because of the hope he brings, we ask you to reach into our past with your saving love, and cleanse us of all that is sinful. Enable us to leave behind that sinful past, letting our gift to you this holy season be our willingness to be made clean by your gift of salvation through Christ our Lord, in whose name we pray. Amen.

Hymns

"Hark! the Herald Angels Sing"
"In the Bleak Midwinter"
"O Come, All Ye Faithful"
"O Little Town of Bethlehem"

CHRISTMAS, SECOND PROPER
(Additional Lessons for Christmas Day)

Gospel: Luke 2:8-20
Theme: Shepherds worship the Christ child

Call to Worship

Pastor: In the simplest bed, and lowliest shelter, the Son of God was born to be our Savior.

People: Humble as his birth was, it was announced by angels who promised his peace to our world.

Pastor: When the shepherds heard the good news, they worshiped Jesus, and then told others what they had seen.

People: We rejoice in God's gift of his Son! May our world accept God's favor, and receive the peace our Savior brings.

Collect

Heavenly Father, who fills our hearts with joy in the birth of your Son: Direct us in our worship to see that in this Christ event, salvation has come into our world. May we share with others, our experience of redemption through Jesus our Savior, in whose name we pray. Amen.

Prayer of Confession

Christmas is important to us, Father. But our joy is so temporary and superficial. We hear the good news of peace; but we are not at peace with ourselves, or with you. Forgive us when we celebrate the gift of your Son, without receiving him as our Savior. Fill us with joy which is genuine, growing out of our Lord's birth in our hearts. In his name we pray. Amen.

Hymns

"Angels, from the Realms of Glory"
"Angels We Have Heard on High"
"It Came Upon the Midnight Clear"
"While Shepherds Watched Their Flocks"

CHRISTMAS, THIRD PROPER
(Additional Lessons for Christmas Day)

First Lesson: Isaiah 52:7-10
Theme: Rejoice in God's salvation

Call to Worship
Pastor: Can you hear what's being said in the midst of all the clamor?
People: God has spoken clearly. He has come to rescue us from the power of sin.
Pastor: God has indeed won the victory. Christ is born, and we are free!
People: May all the world see what mighty works God has done. Christ is for the whole world, our newborn King. Hallelujah!

Collect
Almighty God, you have sent us the good news of your victory over sin! Release our lips from their silent praises; that we may shout with those who know the joy of being rescued from sin through the grace of our Lord Jesus Christ, in whose name we pray. Amen.

Prayer of Confession
We cry for victory, Father, for we stand powerless in the face of sin. But we have heard the good news that our victory is won. Forgive us for our sins, and restore us to your fellowship. Then use us as your messengers; that our world may hear that our victory is their victory, too. Thus may our world be brought together in a fellowship of love, united in your kingdom. In Christ's name we pray. Amen.

Hymns
"All My Heart This Night Rejoices"
"Good Christian Men, Rejoice"
"Joy to the World"
"O Come, All Ye Faithful"

CHRISTMAS, THIRD PROPER
(Additional Lessons for Christmas Day)

Second Lesson: Hebrews 1:1-12
Theme: Jesus reflects the brightness of God's glory

Call to Worship

Pastor: We celebrate the birth of Christ, God's Son whom he sent in his own likeness.

People: Through him God created the universe; and through him God redeems the universe.

Pastor: Greater than all which God has created, Jesus, our Savior, is worthy of our worship.

People: All praise to Jesus, God incarnate, born to share with us the glory of God!

Collect

Father in heaven, whose glory you have revealed through your only Son: Shine upon us in our need; that we may experience the joy for which you sent your Son, in whose name we pray. Amen.

Prayer of Confession

We give our devotion to you, Father, because in Christ we see you more clearly. And what we see causes us to come in humility and repentance, seeking your forgiveness; that we might be restored to wholeness. As we come in adoration of our Savior's birth, open our hearts to receive the salvation for which we sing his praises. In his name we pray. Amen.

Hymns

"Angels from the Realms of Glory"
"Infant Holy, Infant Lowly"
"Love Came Down at Christmas"
"O God of Light, Thy Word, a Lamp"

CHRISTMAS, THIRD PROPER
(Additional Lessons for Christmas Day)

Gospel: John 1:1-14
Theme: The eternal Christ

Call to Worship
Pastor: He who was and is, and always will be, became human to reveal the Divine.
People: We worship Jesus, Son of God, and son of man, born to give us second birth.
Pastor: By his power, we receive power to become God's children, because it is God's will.
People: The glory of the only begotten Son of God fills our hearts with praise to God!

Collect
Eternal God, who chose to become human that we might become divine: Inspire us with true belief in your Son; that we may become your children, and enjoy eternity with our Savior, in whose name we pray. Amen.

Prayer of Confession
We know, Father, that there are people who do not receive your Son as their Savior. We do; and are thankful to be called your children. However, we know there are times when we do not live as your children. Forgive us when we deny you as our Father. Rekindle our faith as we celebrate your Son's birth, with a deep conviction to live as your children. In our Savior's name we pray. Amen.

Hymns
"Hark! the Herald Angels Sing"
"Lo, He Comes with Clouds Descending"
"Love Came Down at Christmas"
"O Word of God Incarnate"

FIRST SUNDAY AFTER CHRISTMAS

First Lesson: Isaiah 61:10—62:3
Theme: Rejoice in what God has done

Call to Worship
Pastor: Rejoice in the God of our salvation!
People: He has come to us with victory over the power of sin!
Pastor: He has saved us to be his forever!
People: Like a bride at her wedding; like seeds sprouting in spring; like a torch in the night; God fills us with praise for all he has done!

Collect
Most gracious Father, who has rescued us from the plight of sin, filling our hearts with the joy of victory and salvation: Let the praise we proclaim in your honor be heard around the world; that our Lord's birth may be recognized as a saving hope for all persons. In his name we pray. Amen.

Prayer of Confession
We rejoice in the gift of new life, Father, expressed in the birth of your Son. But we are slow to accept that gift as a new life for ourselves. Forgive us when we sing our songs of praise without accepting your gift for which we praise you. Lead us in a life of victory over sin; that the praise of our lips will echo the praise of our lives. We pray through Christ our Lord. Amen.

Hymns
"Christ, Whose Glory Fills the Skies"
"Joyful, Joyful, We Adore Thee"
"Let All Together Praise Our God"
"Love Divine, All Loves Excelling"

FIRST SUNDAY AFTER CHRISTMAS

Second Lesson: Galatians 4:4-7
Theme: No longer slaves, but children

Call to Worship
Pastor: In God's own time, he sent his Son to release those enslaved to sin.
People: He not only released us, but adopted us as his children.
Pastor: We know we are God's children, because he has given us his Spirit which confirms our adoption.
People: We praise you, Father, for all the blessings you have bestowed upon your children.

Collect
Father in heaven, who sent your Son to claim us as your children: Release us from the power and influence of sin; that we may respond to the bidding of your Spirit, and claim you as our Father, not only with our lips, but with our lives. In your Son's name we pray. Amen.

Prayer of Confession
O God, we call you Father so easily, even to the point of using your name carelessly in vain. Forgive us for the cheap ways in which we address you, and the bold ways in which we rebel as your children. Grant us your Spirit, that when we call you, Father, it will come from our honest commitment to live as your children. We pray through Christ, our Lord. Amen.

Hymns
"Christ Whose Glory Fills the Skies"
"I Know Not How That Bethlehem's Babe"
"O Little Town of Bethlehem"
"What Child Is This"

FIRST SUNDAY AFTER CHRISTMAS

Gospel: Luke 2:22-40
Theme: Jesus presented in the temple

Call to Worship

Pastor: When the infant Jesus was brought to the temple for dedication, he was received as God's promised messiah.
People: He was regarded as one who would be a light to the Gentiles, and give glory to the Israelites.
Pastor: He received praise, because devout worshipers could see in Jesus their hopes fulfilled.
People: May our devotion to God enable us to see our hopes fulfilled in Jesus, who has come to set us free.

Collect

Gracious Father, whose Son was born to set us free in fulfillment of your promise to all people: Cause our hearts to be receptive to his deliverance, that we may enjoy the salvation for which our souls thirst. In our Savior's name we pray. Amen.

Prayer of Confession

Our hearts become anxious at times, Father, because we feel defeated, or discouraged, or even destroyed. We long for deliverance that will fill our hearts with joy. Forgive us in our depression for not being able to see in Jesus the fulfillment of our highest hope. Open our eyes and hearts to his ministry, that we may know his birth is the answer to our needs. In his name we pray. Amen.

Hymns

"Christ, Whose Glory Fills the Skies"
"Hope of the World"
"Light of the World, We Hail Thee"
"O Morning Star, How Fair and Bright"

JANUARY 1
(When observed as New Year)

First Lesson: Ecclesiastes 3:1-13
Theme: God puts all things in order

Call to Worship

Pastor: The new year comes as an inspiration to begin again in cooperation with God.
People: Life often seems full of confusion. But God breaks through our confession and puts all things in order.
Pastor: He does that through Christ, who came to reveal both God's redemption and judgment.
People: We are in God's hands. May he give order to our lives in this new year as we commit ourselves to Christ.

Collect

O God our Father, who brings order to our lives confused by sin: Let this new year be a time when we follow your order; that sin may no longer distort the path you would have us follow. In our Savior's name we pray. Amen.

Prayer of Confession

Heavenly Father, we are too easily distracted by superficial and sensual attractions. Forgive us for the chaos and confusion of our sinful nature. Reorder our lives at the beginning of this new year, by the gift of your Son; that we may know your will, and surrender our will to yours. We pray through Christ our Lord. Amen.

Hymns

"Come, Let Us Use the Grace Divine"
"O God, Our Help in Ages Past"
"O Happy Day"
"Truehearted, Wholehearted"

JANUARY 1
(When observed as New Year)

Second Lesson: Collossians 2:1-7
Theme: Be strong in Christ

Call to Worship
Pastor: The new year becomes happy when we live it in union with Christ.
People: We welcome this new year, confident that God will lead us in the ways of his Son.
Pastor: May we all continue to grow in our faith as we confirm our loyalty to Christ.
People: We pledge our loyalty to Christ, and thank God for the gift of this new year to grow in our love for him.

Collect
Gracious Father, who has come to us in your Son, Jesus, to show yourself more clearly to us: Strengthen our faith as we strive to be better Christians; that this new year may be a spiritual journey in which we will grow in our love, and in our commitment to our Savior, through whom we pray. Amen.

Prayer of Confession
We accept your Son as Lord, Father, but we have difficulty living in union with him. Forgive us when we have resisted his presence in our lives to go our own way. Help us to begin a new life in this new year in which we will grow spiritually and experience real unity with Christ Jesus our Lord, in whose name we pray. Amen.

Hymns
"All Praise to Thee, for Thou, O King Divine"
"Come, Christians, Join to Sing"
"O Guide to Every Child"
"Take the Name of Jesus with You"

JANUARY 1
(When observed as New Year)

Gospel: Matthew 9:14-17
Theme: Let the new year be new

Call to Worship
Pastor: We have a gift from God: a new year to enjoy life with all its joys.
People: We look forward to each new year when we can start over with our intentions to be better Christians.
Pastor: We are challenged to start this new year without the influence of this past year.
People: With God's help we will let the past year be past, and join with God in a new adventure!

Collect
Heavenly Father, who constantly creates newness of life with opportunities for rebirth and growth: Release us from all that would keep this new year from being a new beginning for us; that we may experience new life in fellowship with your Son, our Lord, in whose name we pray. Amen.

Prayer of Confession
We beg your forgiveness, Father, for all in our lives that have hindered our relationship with you. We ask that you help us begin this year as a new chapter in our lives unaffected by what we have been in the past. Fill us with your Spirit, crowding out whatever there is in our nature that would keep us from growing in accordance with your will. In our Savior's name we pray. Amen.

Hymns
"Be Thou My Vision"
"Dear Master, in Whose Life I See"
"Lead Kindly Light"
"O Come, and Dwell in Me"

SECOND SUNDAY AFTER CHRISTMAS

First Lesson: Jeremiah 31:7-14
Theme: Rejoice because of what the Lord has done

Call to Worship

Pastor: Rejoice in God's gift of salvation which he has made known to us in his Son, Jesus!

People: We praise God because he has come to us with victory over sin, and deliverance to new life!

Pastor: God has reached out to us in love as a father who cares for his children, and a shepherd who guards his flock.

People: We rejoice because of all that God has done for us through his Son, our Savior. All glory and honor be his!

Collect

Glorious Father, whose love has brought such wonderful blessings to us through the gift of your Son: Accept the glad songs of praise we sing to you for saving us, that the joy we feel may give glory and honor to you for all you have done for us. In our Savior's name we pray. Amen.

Prayer of Confession

Father, you have come to us with the wonderful blessings of pure love, renewed life, and victory over sin. Yet we so quickly withdraw from the excitement of Christmas. Forgive us for abusing these blessings you have expressed in Jesus. Help us to return your love by living a new life with Christ, that we may be victorious over sin and give evidence to your great power. We pray through Christ our Lord. Amen.

Hymn

"Christ, Whose Glory Fills the Skies"
"Joyful, Joyful, We Adore Thee"
"Let All Together Praise Our God"
"Love Divine, All Loves Excelling"

SECOND SUNDAY AFTER CHRISTMAS

Second Lesson: Ephesians 1:3-6, 15-18
Theme: Praise God for his grace

Call to Worship
Pastor: Long before we were born, God decided that through his Son he would make us his children.
People: Through Christ, God has blessed us with his fatherly love and benevolent grace.
Pastor: Let us praise God for the gift of his Son, and the grace he gives so freely.
People: We praise you, O God, for sending us your Son who has revealed your grace sufficient to cover our sins.

Collect
Gracious Father, who has chosen us to be your children in spite of our sins: Give us receptive hearts to your Son; that your grace may not have been given in vain through any negligence or refusal on our part. We pray in our Savior's name. Amen.

Prayer of Confession
Were it not for your grace, O God, we would be as winter without the hope of spring. But we know you do not treat us as we deserve. And so we ask for your forgiveness, that we may experience your grace, your cleansing, and your guidance. Refresh us with new life, that we might give a true witness to the power of your grace. In Christ's name we pray. Amen.

Hymns
"Amazing Grace"
"Come, Let Us Use the Grace Divine"
"How Happy Every Child of Grace"
"I Know Not How That Bethlehem's Babe"

SECOND SUNDAY AFTER CHRISTMAS

Gospel: John 1:1-18
Theme: Children of the covenant

Call to Worship
Pastor: Jesus has come as God's Word made flesh, that we may become God's children, born of his Spirit.
People: Our Lord comes to each generation to share God's love and gift of new life.
Pastor: All who receive Jesus are brought into a covenant relationship with God, reborn as his children.
People: We affirm our faith in God our Father, whose covenant love makes us his children.

Collect
Eternal God our Father, whose divine power has made your Word become flesh, and who enables children of flesh to be born of your Spirit: Cause the light and life of Christ to find acceptance in our hearts, that we may begin a new life in covenant with you. We pray through Christ, our Savior. Amen.

Prayer of Confession
Jesus is no stranger to us, Father; but we are weak in the response we make to him. We want to receive him, but it is difficult to reject all that hinders our rebirth. Forgive us for living as if we were only observers of the new covenant you offer through Christ. Take control of our hearts, that we may begin this new year firmly established as children of your covenant. In our Savior's name we pray. Amen.

Hymns
"At the Name of Jesus"
"Love Divine, All Loves Excelling"
"O Come, and Dwell in Me"
"Spirit of God, Descend"

THE EPIPHANY

First Lesson: Isaiah 60:1-6
Theme: The brightness of his presence

Call to Worship
Pastor: God's light shines upon our world to lead us out of the darkness of sin.
People: The brightness of God's presence in Christ reveals our sin, but also his love.
Pastor: God's revelation in Christ is his gift to the whole world. All are invited to receive his love.
People: We praise God for his Son, who is the Savior of our World!

Collect
Almighty God, whose salvation comes as a light into our dark world of sin: Let your light shine through the witness of your church; that all may see your glory in our world today, and come to rejoice in your good news of salvation. In our Savior's name we pray. Amen.

Prayer of Confession
We rejoice in the glory of Christ your Son, who brings your light into our world, Father. But we confess we confine your light to our lives, leaving others in darkness. Forgive us when we abuse your glory possessively rather than sharing it as a gift for our world. Use us as messengers of your salvation; that our world may be brought to your Son, in whose name we pray. Amen.

Hymns
"Break Forth, O Living Light of God"
"Christ Is the World's True Light"
"Christ Whose Glory Fills the Skies"
"Light of the World We Hail Thee"

THE EPIPHANY

Second Lesson: Ephesians 3:1-12
Theme: Gentiles share in God's promises

Call to Worship
Pastor: God has expressed himself in Jesus; and that expression is God's revelation of salvation for all people!
People: We worship God, knowing he loves everyone equally.
Pastor: The divisions we create by pride and prejudice are broken down by God's all-inclusive love.
People: We praise God for sending his Son, Jesus, to be Savior of all persons in our world.

Collect
Father in heaven, who invites all persons to enjoy your promise of redemption though Christ Jesus: Inspire your church to proclaim your message of salvation to all persons; that we may not be guilty of preventing anyone from receiving the good news of Christ, through whom we pray. Amen.

Prayer of Confession
Personal prejudices are such a problem with us, Father. We categorize people without cause, accepting some, and rejecting others. Some we regard as friends in Christ, others we just ignore. Forgive us when we build walls around your church which attempt to keep Christ in, or those he came to save, out. Give us the joy of overcoming the barriers our human nature creates, that we may share the good news of Christ with everyone. In his name we pray. Amen.

Hymns
"Heralds of Christ"
"In Christ There Is No East or West"
"Jesus, United by Thy Grace"

THE EPIPHANY

Gospel: Matthew 2:1-12
Theme: The visit of the wise men

Call to Worship

Pastor: Lift up your hearts, and see the wondrous revelation God gives to our world!
People: We are all on a long journey through life, and are searching for divine guidance.
Pastor: God is pointing the way to salvation by leading us to his Son, the Savior of our world!
People: We, too, have seen his star, and join the throngs who come to worship him!

Collect

Heavenly Father, who reaches into every dark corner of our world with the light of your love in Christ: Guide us in our pilgrimage through life to your Son, Jesus, that we may find the peace and joy for which our souls are searching. In his name we pray. Amen.

Prayer of Confession

We stumble through life from one day to the next, Father. And how like the Israelites' journey in the wilderness our pilgrimage becomes. We are searching for answers to questions about life, and our search seems to be without end. Forgive us when we fail to respond to your guidance which leads us to Christ. Give us directions, as vivid as a star in the sky; that following, we may find our Savior and give him our devotion. In his name we pray. Amen.

Hymns

"As with Gladness Men of Old"
"Brightest and Best"
"Light of the World We Hail Thee"
"We Three Kings"

BAPTISM OF THE LORD
(First Sunday after Epiphany)

First Lesson: Genesis 1:1-5
Theme: Light for our lives

Call to Worship
Pastor: Life at times feels like a darkness that surrounds us, enveloping us in a starless night.
People: Life can also feel like the brightness of a new day enlightened by a rising sun!
Pastor: God our creator continues to create new life, transforming our darkness by the light of his Son.
People: We praise God for his Son, in whom we see God's plan of redemption for us.

Collect
Heavenly Father, who sent your Son to cast out the darkness of sin from our lives: Enlighten us through the ministry of your Son; that we may experience the creation of a new nature which is committed to your will for us. In our Savior's name we pray. Amen.

Prayer of Confession
Eternal God, you have anointed your Son to be a light to lead us in our living. But in that light, we see ourselves, and our unworthiness. Forgive us for all that perpetuates the darkness in our lives. Cleanse us of our sins, and help us to follow in the way your Son would direct us; that we may rejoice in the glory of your love. In our Savior's name we pray. Amen.

Hymns
"Break Forth, O Living Light of God"
"Christ Is the World's True Light"
"Christ, Whose Glory Fills the Skies"
"Walk in the Light"

BAPTISM OF THE LORD
(First Sunday after Epiphany)

Second Lesson: Acts 19:1-7
Theme: Baptism of the Holy Spirit

Call to Worship
Pastor: The rites and rituals of our worship have their place, but they also have their limits.
People: Without a commitment to Christ, our worship has little purpose.
Pastor: It is the Holy Spirit that moves us to commit our lives to Christ.
People: Thanks be to God for the gift of his Spirit that fills our lives with his love and moves us to accept his Son.

Collect
Father in heaven, who blesses us with your Spirit, giving us inspiration, guidance and support: Fill us with your Holy Spirit; that we may live in harmony with your will, and know the joy of the spirit filled life. In the name of Christ we pray. Amen.

Prayer of Confession
It is so easy, Father, for us to get preoccupied with the life of the church, that we miss the power of Christ in living. Forgive us when we avoid the presence and guidance of your Spirit in our lives. Baptize us anew with your Spirit; that we may be empowered to live faithfully in accordance with your will. In our Savior's name we pray. Amen.

Hymns
"Breathe on Me, Breath of God"
"Holy Spirit, Truth Divine"
"O Spirit of the Living God"
"Spirit of God, Descend upon My Heart"

BAPTISM OF THE LORD
(First Sunday after Epiphany)

Gospel: Mark 1:4-11
Theme: Jesus' baptism

Call to Worship
Pastor: Jesus began his ministry blessed by God who anointed him with the Holy Spirit.
People: We worship Jesus who came as God's anointed Servant to be our Lord.
Pastor: Jesus accepted his role as God's Servant, making his ministry a revelation of God's redemption.
People: May our devotion to Christ bring the blessing of God's Spirit into our lives with the assurance of salvation from sin.

Collect
Almighty God, who anointed Jesus to be your Servant, and commissioned him with a saving ministry: Baptize us with your Holy Spirit through the ministry of Jesus; that we may experience the salvation which you have proclaimed through your Servant, in whose name we pray. Amen.

Prayer of Confession
We are believers in Christ, Father, who know Jesus came as your Servant to minister on our behalf. But we still live as though we were responsible only to ourselves, and Jesus' ministry becomes a gospel which we read without taking to heart. Forgive us when we resist the saving influence of your Holy Spirit by ignoring the purpose for which you anointed your Son. Convince us of the joy of salvation, that we may experience the cleansing from sin which Jesus desires to perform in us. We pray in his name. Amen.

Hymns
"At the Name of Jesus"
"Come, Holy Spirit, Heavenly Dove"
"Jesus, the Name High Over All"
"O Son of God Incarnate"

SECOND SUNDAY AFTER THE EPIPHANY

First Lesson: 1 Samuel 3:1-10, (11-20)
Theme: Samuel's call and response

Call to Worship
Pastor: We have come to God's house. We are in his presence. And he is calling to us.
People: We give our ears, our hearts, and our lives to God to be used in his service.
Pastor: God's call requires the total commitment of living in accordance with his will.
People: We wait for God to speak, anxious to know his will for us.

Collect
O God our Father, who calls your children into obedient service: Speak to us through our expressions of worship, that we may know your will for us and respond with willing hearts. We pray through Christ our Lord. Amen.

Prayer of Confession
When we think about your calling people into service, Father, we usually think of other people. So when you call us, we do not hear, because we feel that is too special for us. Forgive us when we ignore your call, misinterpreting it as an experience for professionals only, or those more spiritual than ourselves. Keep calling until we hear, that we may not miss the life you would have us live in your service. We pray in our Savior's name. Amen.

Hymns
"God Calling Yet"
"Jesus Calls Us O'er the Tumult"
"Master, Speak! Thy Servant Heareth"
"The Voice of God Is Calling"

SECOND SUNDAY AFTER THE EPIPHANY

Second Lesson: 1 Corinthians 6:12-20
Theme: Total commitment

Call to Worship

Pastor: The call of God is a never-ending communication with his children.
People: We are Christians because we have heard God's call to follow Christ.
Pastor: When God calls us into discipleship, he calls for our total being to be surrendered to him.
People: We come in response to God's call, that his Spirit may strengthen us to live the Christian life.

Collect

Almighty God, who calls us into discipleship, demanding the complete surrender of our whole nature: Inspire us with your Spirit; that our response to your call may be a full commitment of body, mind, and soul to the way of Christ our Lord, through whom we pray. Amen.

Prayer of Confession

Father, you have called us into discipleship; but too often we interpret that call as being directed to others, excusing ourselves from responsible behavior. Other times we accept your call but limit it to a particular task instead of a way of life. Forgive us when we avoid your call to live wholly dedicated to the Christian faith. Give us new priorities, and a new sense of discipleship, as we attempt to serve our Lord Jesus Christ, in whose name we pray. Amen.

Hymns

"Breathe on Me, Breath of God"
"Jesus Calls Us"
"Take My Life"
"Take Time to Be Holy"

SECOND SUNDAY AFTER THE EPIPHANY

Gospel: John 1:35-42
Theme: John's followers become Jesus' disciples

Call to Worship
Pastor: The ministry of John the Baptizer pointed to God's Word who became flesh.
People: We, too, would become followers of Jesus, the Word made flesh.
Pastor: In Jesus we find the fullest revelation of God, a revelation which calls for sincere discipleship.
People: May our commitment to Christ enable us to live in a closer relationship with God our Father.

Collect
Gracious Father, who calls your children into faithful devotion through the Lordship of your Son: Make us steadfast in our allegiance to Christ, that we may live in honest commitment to the disciplines of the Christian life. In our Savior's name we pray. Amen.

Prayer of Confession
We have found the Messiah, too, Father, because he has found us. And Jesus has called us to live as his disciples. Forgive us for all expressions in our lifestyles which deny that we are disciples of Christ. Strengthen us in living the Christian life; that our witness may inspire others to come and be found by Jesus, in whose name we pray.

Hymns
"I Am Thine, O Lord"
"I've Found a Friend"
"I Would Be True"
"O Jesus, I Have Promised"

THIRD SUNDAY AFTER THE EPIPHANY

First Lesson: Jonah 3:1-5, 10
Theme: Nineveh repents and is spared

Call to Worship

Pastor: Life may be full of enjoyable experiences; but if those experiences shut God out, we are headed for destruction.

People: We do not deny the reality of God, but it is also true we do promote the reality of sin.

Pastor: God proclaims his message clearly: If we repent, he will save us from the destruction our sins would bring to us.

People: May God help us turn from our sinful ways and acknowledge his presence in our lives.

Collect

Almighty God, who warns your children of judgment, offering salvation if they will turn from their sins: Give us the faith to believe your warning and your mercy; that we may be spared from the evil consequence of our sins, and enjoy the blessing of your grace. We pray through Christ our Redeemer. Amen.

Prayer of Confession

It seems appropriate to talk about repentance in the church, Father, but we pay little attention to its significance. We have restricted it to church vocabulary, so that it will not interfere with the way we live. Forgive us when we have listened to your warning, and then live as if we had no sins from which to turn away. In our daily lives, outside the context of a worship service, convince us of our need to repent, that we may heed your word and receive your forgiveness. In Jesus' name we pray. Amen.

Hymns

"Come, Every Soul by Sin Oppressed"
"God Calling Yet! Shall I Not Hear?"
"Just as I Am, Without One Plea"
"Sinners Turn: Why Will You Die?"

THIRD SUNDAY AFTER THE EPIPHANY

Second Lesson: 1 Corinthians 7:29-31 (32-35)
Theme: Live in expectation of God's Kingdom

Call to Worship
Pastor: We are people with many possessions, many obligations, many involvements.
People: **Life is very complicated, and sometimes we feel as if we are caught up in a riddle without meaning.**
Pastor: We let life tie us down, but God would like us to break free in expectation of his Kingdom. Then life would take on new meaning.
People: **We celebrate the Kingdom of God, and rejoice in our hope of living in that Kingdom!**

Collect
Eternal God, whose Kingdom is the hope of all who put their trust in you: Enable us to live as people who are expecting your Kingdom, that the preoccupations of this life may not prevent us from being ready for your Kingdom. We pray through Christ our Lord. Amen.

Prayer of Confession
We work hard at making a good life, Father. And then all which looked good seems to weight us down as a burden, rather than lift us as a blessing. We become possessed by life instead of possessing it. Forgive us when we live as if this world were an end in itself. Help us to live in preparation for a richer life in your Kingdom with our Lord and Savior, Jesus Christ, in whose name we pray. Amen.

Hymns
"Judge Eternal, Throned in Splendor"
"Lead On, O King Eternal"
"O Day of God, Draw Nigh"
"Take My Life, and Let It Be Consecrated"

THIRD SUNDAY AFTER THE EPIPHANY

Gospel: Mark 1:14-20
Theme: Faith which produces repentance

Call to Worship

Pastor: We believe God's Kingdom is his ultimate expression of love and redemption.
People: We believe God wants each one of us to live in his Kingdom.
Pastor: Such faith motivates us to turn from the sins of this world in preference for his Kingdom.
People: Thanks be to God for the good news he shares through his Son, Jesus!

Collect

Gracious Father, whose Son preached the good news of your Kingdom, and asked us to believe with penitent lives: Grant us the faith to turn from our sins, that we may be accepted in your Kingdom. In our Savior's name we pray. Amen.

Prayer of Confession

We hear the announcement of your Kingdom, Father, but it seems like a dream in the distant future. So even though we profess faith, our life does not reveal much change in direction. Forgive us when our faith is sufficient to herald your Kingdom, but insufficient to change our way of living in preparation for your Kingdom. Strengthen our faith, so we will become strong in our Christian discipleship. We pray through Christ our Lord. Amen.

Hymns

"Come, Let Us, Who in Christ Believe"
"How Can A Sinner Know"
"How Happy Every Child of Grace"
"O For A Faith that Will Not Shrink"

FOURTH SUNDAY AFTER THE EPIPHANY

First Lesson: Deuteronomy 18:15-20
Theme: God promises a prophet

Call to Worship
Pastor: God has sent many prophets to proclaim his message, that we may understand his will.
People: We thank God for giving us understanding through the message of his prophets.
Pastor: Jesus fulfills God's promise of a great prophet who would speak with authority in his name.
People: We give our devotion to Jesus who has authority not only to teach God's will, but to lead us into his presence.

Collect
Almighty God, who has spoken through many prophets, but who has given your Son authority not only to speak in your name, but also to redeem sinners: Open our hearts to his prophetic ministry of redemption; that we may yield to his authority, and receive the salvation which he mediates. In our Savior's name we pray. Amen.

Prayer of Confession
Our Father, we have tuned in to your prophets when we think they are predicting the future. But our minds wander when we hear them telling us how to live in the present. Forgive us when our indifference to your message keeps us from recognizing the authority with which Jesus speaks, as well as the grace by which he saves us. Transform the deafness of our hearts and minds into submission and obedience, that we may respond with faithful discipleship. We pray through Christ our Redeemer. Amen.

Hymns
"Jesus, Thine All-Victorious Love"
"Lord, Speak to Me"
"O Young and Fearless Prophet"
"Talk with Us, Lord"

FOURTH SUNDAY AFTER THE EPIPHANY

Second Lesson: 1 Corinthians 8:1-13
Theme: Be an example for weaker Christians

Call to Worship
Pastor: Christian fellowship requires each member to have concern for each other's spiritual health.
People: Christian faith is nurtured when strong Christians support the weak.
Pastor: Our witness is necessary to support those who may be unsure of their faith.
People: We pray that our witness will not mislead or confuse any who need guidance in their commitment to Christ.

Collect
Almighty God, who provides strength and solidarity in your church by the mutual sharing of faith among Christians: Guide us in our witness, that we may provide support and encouragement to those who look for our example. In Christ's name we pray. Amen.

Prayer of Confession
We are a part of the body of believers, Father; but many times we become independent with our faith, and careless in the witness we give to others who are searching for the truth. Forgive us when we hurt others in their faith by the witness we give to our faith. Unite us in a fellowship of mutual upbuilding in our commitment to Christ, in whose name we pray. Amen.

Hymns
"A Charge to Keep"
"I Would Be True"
"O Brother Man, Fold to Thy Heart"
"O Master, Let Me Walk with Thee"

FOURTH SUNDAY AFTER THE EPIPHANY

Gospel: Mark 1:21-28
Theme: Jesus taught with authority

Call to Worship

Pastor: To worship God is to respond with obedience when he speaks to us.
People: We are God's children, eager to hear what God's will is for us.
Pastor: We can know God's will through the teaching of Jesus, for he spoke with the authority of God.
People: We yield to our Lord's authority, assured that he can cleanse us with his word.

Collect

Father in heaven, whose Son taught with authority which compelled obedience and surrender: Take control of our lives, and cast out all evil which possesses our souls; that we may be free to follow your will. We pray in our Savior's name. Amen.

Prayer of Confession

We love the stories of Jesus, Father, which tell us of love, healing, and forgiveness. But the stories of obedience, discipline, and commitment are not as familiar to us. Forgive us when our freedom to live as we choose convinces us that Jesus has no real authority over us. Cause us to hear Jesus speaking to us with the same authority which casts out demons, that we may be cleansed of all that hinders our devotion to him. In his name we pray. Amen.

Hymns

"I Want A Principle Within"
"Make Me A Captive, Lord"
"Savior, Teach Me Day by Day"
"Take the Name of Jesus with You"

FIFTH SUNDAY AFTER THE EPIPHANY

First Lesson: Job 7:1-7
Theme: Job's misery

Call to Worship

Pastor: Job communicates an important message from God: Misery is not always a punishment for sin, and righteousness does not earn salvation from God.

People: We are slow to learn that we are justified by faith alone, not by any righteousness of ours.

Pastor: In spite of what life brings to us, God does not leave us. His grace is sufficient for each of us.

People: We trust in God to save us by his mercy, and to enable us by his Spirit to live through our trials.

Collect

O God, our heavenly Father, who does not punish us according to our sins, or save us because of our righteousness: Heal our miseries, and forgive our sins; that our lives may reveal your saving grace which you offer to all persons. In our Savior's name we pray. Amen.

Prayer of Confession

We are quick to complain with the slightest misery, Father; and we are eager to witness to our righteous deeds, because we still think in terms of a merit system for salvation. Forgive us when we feel rejected or accepted because of our sins or righteousness, instead of by your grace. Show us your love in Jesus; that we may find healing for our miseries, and mercy for our sins. We pray through Christ our Lord. Amen.

Hymns

"Be Not Dismayed"
"Be Still My Soul"
"Holy Spirit, Faithful Guide"
"Thou Hidden Source of Calm Repose"

FIFTH SUNDAY AFTER THE EPIPHANY

Second Lesson: 1 Corinthians 9:16-23
Theme: Paul demonstrates the gospel

Call to Worship
Pastor: Christ crucified is a miracle of salvation for everyone!
People: We come to hear the good news of Christ, that we may rejoice in our salvation.
Pastor: Our ministry is to share the gospel in such a way that all may be able to understand the miracle of their salvation.
People: We pray that God will use his church in a pluralistic ministry which communicates his gospel to all people.

Collect
Gracious Father, who requires your church to be all things to all people in order to reach everyone with your message of salvation: Make us willing to be used in your service, that we may become the living gospel which others will understand and accept. We pray through Christ our Lord. Amen.

Prayer of Confession
We know there is an endless variety of personalities, Father, to which we must interpret the gospel. But we become exclusive, and selective, shutting many out because of their differences and our indifference. Forgive us for our narrow ministry which we have considered to be our faithful service. Broaden our horizons, and our abilities, as we reach out in love to share your love with all kinds of people. In Jesus' name we pray. Amen.

Hymns
"I Love to Tell the Story"
"O Master, Let Me Walk with Thee"
"Rescue the Perishing"
"Where Cross the Crowded Ways of Life"

FIFTH SUNDAY AFTER THE EPIPHANY

Gospel: Mark 1:29-39
Theme: The miracle of redemption — for everyone

Call to Worship
Pastor: Many people followed Jesus because of his miracles, but we follow him because of his crucifixion.
People: Jesus healed many people, but his greatest miracle took place on the cross for everyone.
Pastor: Jesus continues to heal the weak and brokenhearted with his miracle on the cross.
People: We worship our living Lord, who suffered death on the cross to heal the infirmities by which sin cripples us.

Collect
Merciful Father, whose Son brings healing to our wounded souls by his death on the cross: Touch our broken lives with the miracle of forgiveness, that we may be restored to a life of joy and thanksgiving. In Jesus' name we pray. Amen.

Prayer of Confession
Diseases still attack our bodies, Father, and we long for a miracle worker who could heal us. We read of the miracles of Jesus, and wish it would happen today more often. But we forget the real miracle for which Jesus came, that took place on the cross, and does bring healing to wounded souls. Forgive us for wanting something less than what Jesus is able to give. Help us to give ourselves in full surrender, that his death on the cross will make us whole. In our Savior's name we pray. Amen.

Hymns
"Amazing Grace"
"Jesus Is All the World to Me"
"Pass Me Not, O Gentle Savior"
"There Is A Balm in Gilead"

SIXTH SUNDAY AFTER THE EPIPHANY
(Proper 1)

First Lesson: 2 Kings 5:1-14
Theme: Elisha heals Naaman

Call to Worship
Pastor: Leprosy was once a dreaded skin disease that separated those afflicted from family and friends.
People: **The Bible tells us of many who by faith were healed of that dreaded disease.**
Pastor: Would that we were as anxious to be cleansed of the spiritual disease, sin, and be restored to fellowship with God.
People: **We rejoice in the healing power that God shares with us through Christ!**

Collect
Gracious Father, who comes with love and forgiveness to your children who have become sinful outcasts: Make us clean through the blood of Christ; that we may be restored to your fellowship, and rejoice in your love. We pray through Christ our Lord. Amen.

Prayer of Confession
Sin has made us unclean, Father, but we know your Son comes to heal us. Forgive us for our sins which eat away at the very essence of our being. Make our hearts clean; that we may enjoy the fellowship of your children, and give glory to Jesus our Savior, in whose name we pray. Amen.

Hymns
"Father, I Stretch My Hands to Thee"
"Have Thine Own Way, Lord"
"I Heard the Voice of Jesus Say"
"Pass Me Not, O Gentle Savior"

SIXTH SUNDAY AFTER THE EPIPHANY
(Proper 1)

Second Lesson: 1 Corinthians 9:24-27
Theme: Let your life manifest Christ

Call to Worship

Pastor: The Christian life is a challenge to be a personal representative of Christ in all situations.

People: The Christian life is made difficult by rules and regulations, but also by the absence of rules and regulations in some situations.

Pastor: When we are in doubt as to how to witness, the rule is to do our best to live as Christ would.

People: We trust in God's Spirit to lead us in our example of what we believe to be his will.

Collect

Father in heaven, who knows the confusion and differences of your children as we share our faith: Enable us by your Spirit to demonstrate the life of Christ in our witness; that we may not lead anyone astray by misinterpreting our commitment to Jesus our Lord, through whom we pray. Amen.

Prayer of Confession

Our Father, there are times when we wonder why people feel the way they do as Christians. We are Christians, too, but do not feel the convictions they feel. Forgive us when we argue with them, or when we weaken their faith by the example we set. Give us the grace to let our witness be a demonstration of Jesus' life, rather than a contest between our convictions of what is right or what is wrong. In our Savior's name we pray. Amen.

Hymns

"A Charge to Keep I Have"
"All Praise to Our Redeeming Lord"
"I Would Be True"

SIXTH SUNDAY AFTER THE EPIPHANY
(Proper 1)

Gospel: Mark 1:40-45
Theme: A Messiah more than a miracle worker

Call to Worship
Pastor: People whom Jesus healed were so thrilled that they could not keep quiet about the miracle!
People: Jesus usually told them not to say anything about it, but they would not listen to him.
Pastor: Christ came to heal everyone from the cross; but we tend to witness more to lesser miracles, instead of shouting the good news of salvation.
People: Praise God for all he does through Jesus! May our joy point to the great miracle of forgiveness which Jesus offers to all from Calvary.

Collect
Almighty God, who sent your Son to our world to give forgiveness and healing of souls: Keep our daily blessings from becoming ends in themselves, but rather signs of the great miracle you want to perform in us; that we may come to Calvary, and be saved by Christ our Redeemer, through whom we pray. Amen.

Prayer of Confession
Faith healing thrills us, Father, along with many other miraculous blessings. And in our praise, we fail to see that these are illustrations of the greatest miracle: the healing of souls. Forgive us when we have more joy for the healing of a diseased body than for lost souls restored at Calvary. Lead us in a ministry which will point others to what Christ will do for them, that salvation may continue to be a daily miracle. We pray in Jesus' name. Amen.

Hymns
"Hope of the World"
"O God, Whose Will Is Life"
"Rescue the Perishing"
"We've A Story to Tell to the Nations"

SEVENTH SUNDAY AFTER THE EPIPHANY
(Proper 2)

First Lesson: Isaiah 43:18-25
Theme: God's ever-new deliverance

Call to Worship
Pastor: God has done many wonderful things in history for his people.
People: We know of many wonderful things God has done for us, too; and we praise him for each one.
Pastor: The good news is that God has come in a new way with deliverance from sin through Jesus Christ, opening a glorious future for us.
People: We look forward to our final reward of being blessed in God's Kingdom for eternity.

Collect
Glorious Father, who does not leave your children to survive only on memories of past blessings, but continues to provide deliverance from sin with the joy of new blessings: Confirm our hope in tomorrow, that we may live in the assurance that you are going before us. We pray through Christ our Lord. Amen.

Prayer of Confession
We cherish experiences of the past in which you made your presence known to us, Father. We sometimes wish we could relive them. But such memories hold us back from receiving the glorious future where you would lead us. Forgive us when we prevent ourselves from receiving new experiences of deliverance and hope by dwelling on the past. Come into our lives in a fresh way, that the joy of your forgiveness will always be a new experience for us. In Jesus' name we pray. Amen.

Hymns
"All the Way My Savior Leads Me"
"God of Our Life"
"How Great Thou Art"
"We Come Unto Our Fathers' God"

SEVENTH SUNDAY AFTER THE EPIPHANY
(Proper 2)

Second Lesson: 2 Corinthians 1:18-22
Theme: The gospel affirms God's promises

Call to Worship

Pastor: The gospel is an affirmation that God is true to his Word. His promises are fulfilled in Jesus.

People: We praise God who is faithful to his children! We know we can depend on him.

Pastor: God calls us to affirm his gospel with lives which give a faithful witness to his salvation.

People: May our lives become a resounding "Amen!" to the love of God expressed in Jesus Christ.

Collect

Most gracious Father, whose inspiration of hope is made firm in the Good News of Jesus: Help us to live in faithfulness to the gospel, that we may affirm your gift of salvation as the source of our hope. We pray through Christ our Lord. Amen.

Prayer of Confession

We have no doubts, Father, that you keep your promises. We read the gospel of Christ, and feel your love flooding our souls. But, our lives, which ought to affirm that Good News, are often unsure; and we do not always give a true affirmation of salvation in Jesus. Forgive us when we waver between sincere commitment and apathetic indifference. Make us strong in our faith, that we may be consistent with a true witness to our Savior's love. In his name we pray. Amen.

Hymns

"I Am Thine, O Lord"
"Lord Jesus, I Love Thee"
"O For A Thousand Tongues to Sing"
"O Jesus, I Have Promised"

SEVENTH SUNDAY AFTER THE EPIPHANY
(Proper 2)

Gospel: Mark 2:1-12
Theme: Jesus' authority to forgive

Call to Worship
Pastor: Early in Jesus' ministry he was manifested as God's Servant who had authority to forgive sins.
People: The message Jesus taught, and the miracles he performed, all illustrate his mission to save.
Pastor: His mission is also illustrated in the rejection which Jesus met, because it foreshadows the cross by which Jesus gives salvation.
People: We open our hearts to Jesus' authority to forgive our sins which have made his cross necessary for us.

Collect
Most merciful Father, who gave your Son authority to forgive sins: Have mercy on us in our sinful condition, that we may experience the healing of forgiveness which your Son came to share with us. In his name we pray. Amen.

Prayer of Confession
We do not question Jesus' right to forgive the sinner, Father. We know that is why he came. Yet we still hold on to sins which we want the right to commit. Forgive us when we resist the healing in our souls for which Jesus came. Help us to surrender ourselves to the authority which Jesus has, that we may be made whole to praise your name. We pray through Christ our Lord. Amen.

Hymns
"Come, Every Soul by Sin Oppressed"
"Dear Lord and Father of Mankind"
"I Am Coming to the Cross"
"I Heard the Voice of Jesus Say"

EIGHTH SUNDAY AFTER THE EPIPHANY
(Proper 3)

First Lesson: Hosea 2:14-20
Theme: God takes the initiative to forgive

Call to Worship
Pastor: God knows where we are when we let sin lead us astray.
People: It is too easy for us to be distracted from total commitment to our Lord.
Pastor: Sinful as we may become, God never stops trying to win us back with his love.
People: We thank God for having the mercy needed to forgive our unfaithfulness.

Collect
Gracious Father, who comes to us with love in our sinful waywardness: Make us your people once again, through the grace of your Son, Jesus Christ; that we may be glad to claim you as our God. In our Savior's name we pray. Amen.

Prayer of Confession
We know what it is to feel lost and disowned because of sin, our Father. And we thank you for your constant love with which you reach out to us in mercy. Forgive us for our sins which have caused us to be unfaithful to you. Accept our repentance, and take us back as your people to live in the blessing of your faithfulness to us. We pray through Christ our Redeemer. Amen.

Hymns
"Amazing Grace"
"Come, Thou Fount of Every Blessing"
"Depth of Mercy"
"I Sought the Lord"

EIGHTH SUNDAY AFTER THE EPIPHANY
(Proper 3)

Second Lesson: 2 Corinthians 3:1-6
Theme: Ability to serve comes from God

Call to Worship
Pastor: God depends on the people of his church to be effective in winning converts to Christ.
People: We are glad for the many converts which the church has won over the years through its missionary and evangelistic endeavors.
Pastor: But none of us can boast of our own success. It is God who enables us to be effective in our service.
People: We trust God to enable us in our ministry to give him honor and glory through the fruit of our labors.

Collect
Almighty God, whose power is the source of strength in the ministry of your church: Enable us in our witness and service; that we may turn the hearts of many to the loving grace of your Son, Jesus, in whose name we pray. Amen.

Prayer of Confession
We want your church to grow, Father, because it is a means of sharing your love in Christ Jesus with our world. But in our ambition, we measure success or failure in terms of what we do or do not do. Forgive us when we feel we are self-sufficient in being your church in action. Forgive us when we have failed, because we ignore your power. Give us a great harvest by the power of your Spirit working through us. We pray in Jesus' name. Amen.

Hymns
"Christ Is Made the Sure Foundation"
"Come, Thou Almighty King"
"God of Grace and God of Glory"
"The Church's One Foundation"

EIGHTH SUNDAY AFTER THE EPIPHANY
(Proper 3)

Gospel: Mark 2:18-22
Theme: The old and new wineskins

Call to Worship
Pastor: God has done a new thing in Christ. His grace and mercy have broken through the power of sin with salvation!

People: How often we become set in our ways, and make it difficult for God to break through with his love!

Pastor: God has created us to be living beings, necessitating growth. And that is true of our spiritual life, too!

People: May we be open to the creative work of God revealing his constant love to us.

Collect
Eternal God, who is ever at work to make your redemptive love known to us: Keep us alive as growing persons in body, mind, and spirit, that we may be receptive to any new revelation of your presence in our midst. We pray through Christ our Lord. Amen.

Prayer of Confession
We are familiar with our past, Father, and that makes us secure in our faith. But it also makes us resist new adventures in faith which you constantly provide through your Spirit. Forgive us when we have more confidence in our past than in your presence. Break through the rigid molds of our Christian experience, and expand our faith as your Spirit leads. In our Savior's name we pray. Amen.

Hymns
"God Moves In A Mysterious Way"
"Open My Eyes, That I May See"
"O Spirit of the Living God"
"Through All the Changing Scenes of Life"

LAST SUNDAY AFTER THE EPIPHANY
(The Transfiguration of the Lord)

First Lesson: 2 Kings 2:1-12a
Theme: Elisha sees Elijah taken up to heaven

Call to Worship

Pastor: God reveals his glory to those who are persistent in their loyalty and faithfulness.

People: We have experienced great blessings because of God's glory. But we know God has an even greater glory for those who are faithful.

Pastor: We are called to serve in the present, but we are strengthened by our hope in a future glory which God has revealed in Christ.

People: We thank God for revealing his glory in Christ who gives us hope in God's eternal power.

Collect

Eternal God, who shares the glory of your nature with those who commit themselves to you in true devotion: Make us steadfast in our love and service, that we may be encouraged by the experience of hope which your glory gives. We pray through Christ our Lord. Amen.

Prayer of Confession

We want to be your followers, Father, but we are easily distracted from our loyalty. We know we prevent ourselves from many wonderful experiences because of our weak commitment. Forgive us when our discipleship is hindered by interests outside, and contradictory to, our faith. Give us persistence which will keep us in your presence, and love which will keep us in your service. We pray in Jesus' name. Amen.

Hymns

"A Charge to Keep I Have"
"Are Ye Able"
"Dear Master, in Whose Life I See"
"O Splendor of God's Glory Bright"

LAST SUNDAY AFTER THE EPIPHANY
(The Transfiguration of the Lord)

Second Lesson: 2 Corinthians 4:3-6
Theme: God's self-revelation through his Spirit

Call to Worship
Pastor: God gives us his Spirit that enables us to know Jesus as our Lord and Savior.
People: We look to Jesus, and the more we turn to him, the more we become like him.
Pastor: It is only through our Lord that we are able to know God and respond to his love.
People: We are anxious to learn more of Jesus, that our hearts and minds may be opened to the love of God.

Collect
Gracious God, our heavenly Father, whose Spirit reveals to us the nature of your Son: Draw us close to Christ, that in his presence our lives may reflect his glory, and be transformed into his likeness. In his name we pray. Amen.

Prayer of Confession
Father, we would turn to Jesus, but not often enough. Our communication with him tends to be too infrequent to experience the transformation in our lives you want us to have. Forgive us for hiding behind the veils of shallow faith, weak commitment, and selfish living. Cause your Spirit to reveal our Savior to us in such a way that we may remain in his presence, until his glory becomes a part of our new creation. We pray in his name. Amen.

Hymns
"God of All Power and Truth and Grace"
"I Want a Principle Within"
"Jesus, Thine All-Victorious Love"
"Lord, I Want to Be a Christian"
"Love Divine, All Loves Excelling"
"O Come, and Dwell in Me."

LAST SUNDAY AFTER THE EPIPHANY
(The Transfiguration of the Lord)

Gospel: Mark 9:2-9
Theme: Jesus' transfiguration

Call to Worship

Pastor: Our Lord's glory was manifested through his transfiguration in a mountaintop experience.

People: God clearly revealed that Jesus was his Son, and had a divine mission.

Pastor: That mission included a cross. So the disciples were charged not to share what they had seen until after Jesus' resurrection.

People: We praise God for his glorious Son, whose life, death, and resurrection fulfilled his redemptive mission.

Collect

Almighty God, who revealed your divine nature in the ministry of Jesus Christ whose glory on the mountain manifested the atoning grace of his death on the cross: Reveal the salvation which Christ provides for us; that we may receive him as Lord and Savior, and honor him with our lives. In his name we pray. Amen.

Prayer of Confession

We worship a risen Savior, Father, who shares his glory in our lives. But there are times when we forget that Christ came into his glory only by way of the cross. Forgive us for our sins which made it necessary for Christ to go to the cross in order to bring us into his glory. Help us to live as redeemed people who have been with our Lord not only on the mountain, but at the cross. In our Savior's name we pray. Amen.

Hymns

"All Hail the Power of Jesus' Name"
"Crown Him with Many Crowns"
"Joyful, Joyful, We Adore Thee"
"O Son of God Incarnate"

ASH WEDNESDAY

First Lesson: Joel 2:1-2, 12-17a
Theme: God is merciful to the penitent

Call to Worship
Pastor: God knows that while we are people of faith, we are not always people with faith.
People: It is so easy to take faith for granted, and consequently live contrary to the faith we profess.
Pastor: If we are sincere about faith, then let us return to God in true repentance, and begin a new life.
People: We have confidence in God's mercy, and seek his forgiveness for our insincerity.

Collect
Most merciful Father, who calls us to you in sincere and complete devotion: Share your love with us as we return to you in full surrender; that we may know your forgiveness and give you our allegiance. In our Savior's name we pray. Amen.

Prayer of Confession
This is not our first prayer to you, Father, yet so many of our prayers have been religious words instead of honest thoughts. Forgive us when we have only pretended with our religious rituals. Set us in a new direction in our faith journey; that our daily living may be our true worship. In Christ's name we pray. Amen.

Hymns
"Have Thine Own Way"
"Just As I Am"
"More Love to Thee, O Christ"
"Out of the Depths I Cry to Thee"

ASH WEDNESDAY

Second Lesson: 2 Corinthians 5:20b-6:2
Theme: Don't waste God's grace

Call to Worship

Pastor: Sin separates us from God, but God's grace is sufficient to restore us in love.
People: How great is God's grace to make friends even of us!
Pastor: Don't let God's grace go unused in your life. Say yes to him, and rejoice in his love.
People: We confess our sinfulness; but we also confess our faith in God's grace.

Collect

Gracious heavenly Father, who is always at work making friends of those whom sin has molded into enemies: Be gracious unto us; that we may rejoice in the salvation offered through your only Son, in whose name we pray. Amen.

Prayer of Confession

Why do you listen to us, Father, when we have denied your love with our sins? Only because of your marvelous grace! And how much we need that. Forgive us for wanting you, without wanting to be yours. Let your grace refresh us anew and restore us in love; that we may love you as much as we are loved by you. In the name of Christ we pray. Amen.

Hymns

"Amazing Grace"
"Come, Every Soul by Sin Oppressed"
"I Am Coming to the Cross"
"I Gave My Life for Thee"

ASH WEDNESDAY

Gospel: Matthew 6:1-6, 16-21
Theme: Our piety is to please God

Call to Worship
Pastor: To be a follower of Christ is to produce Christian behavior.
People: We certainly want the way we live to reflect the faith we believe.
Pastor: But we must be careful that what we do brings glory to God, not praise to ourselves.
People: May our lives, our faith, our love, and our service give God the glory he deserves.

Collect
Heavenly Father, who depends on our witness to lead others into your kingdom: Inspire us to be faithful and honest in our lifestyle; that others, instead of seeing our good works, will see your Son revealed through us. In his name we pray. Amen.

Prayer of Confession
We want to do good works, Father, because we love you. But we confess there are times when we like what others say about our devotion. Forgive us when we have enjoyed such praise. Help us to learn how to live a righteous life without letting our piety become a public demonstration. In Jesus' name we pray. Amen.

Hymns
"Be Thou My Vision"
"Forth in Thy Name"
"I Want a Principle Within"
"I Would Be True"

FIRST SUNDAY OF LENT

First Lesson: Genesis 9:8-17
Theme: God's covenant of preservation

Call to Worship

Pastor: God has made a covenant with all people, promising never to destroy the earth with a flood.
People: We often see his rainbow in the sky as a sign of that promise.
Pastor: God would rather redeem his world than destroy it, even though we rebel in sin.
People: We celebrate God's saving love with which he floods our sinful world!

Collect

Almighty God, whose love preserves us from being destroyed by sin: Convince us of the mercy expressed in your love, that we may turn from our wicked ways and live in fellowship with you. We pray through Christ our Lord. Amen.

Prayer of Confession

We abuse your love, Father, with our sinful ways. Like the unbelieving neighbors of Noah, who took lightly the consequence of sin, we too, feel safe in our worldly pleasures. Forgive us when we refuse to change our ways, unmoved by your patient and merciful love. Keep us in your covenant, assured of your protection, but also responsible for our faithfulness to you. In our Savior's name we pray. Amen.

Hymns

"All People That on Earth Do Dwell"
"Be Still My Soul"
"There's A Wideness in God's Mercy"
"What Shall I Do My God to Love"

FIRST SUNDAY OF LENT

Second Lesson: 1 Peter 3:18-22
Theme: The significance of baptism

Call to Worship
Pastor: Christ, who was sinless, died on our behalf, that we may be raised to new life with God.
People: Our baptism is a witness of Christ's death and resurrection, through which God saves us to that new life.
Pastor: Our baptism also witnesses to our repentance in which we die to sin, and commit ourselves to Christ.
People: Christ has saved us to new life! May our lives give honor and glory to him!

Collect
Gracious God, whose Son gives us new life through his death and resurrection: Affirm in us the faith to which our baptism witnesses, that we may be true to your love with the lives we live. We pray through Christ our Lord. Amen.

Prayer of Confession
Baptism is a sacred rite in our faith, Father. But we show more reverence for the ritual than the witness. Forgive us when we witness to a rebirth of the soul without concern for growing in the new life to which we have been born. Convince us of your cleansing power through baptism, and keep us mindful of our promises, that we may be steadfast in our discipleship. In our Savior's name we pray. Amen.

Hymns
"Alas! and Did My Savior Bleed"
"Come, Every Soul by Sin Oppressed"
"Come, Let Us Rise with Christ"
"Come, Thou Fount of Every Blessing"

FIRST SUNDAY OF LENT

Gospel: Mark 1:9-15
Theme: Jesus' victory over temptation

Call to Worship
Pastor: The symbol of the cross draws us into the presence of God where we receive the gift of salvation in atonement for our sins.
People: The shame of the cross has become our glory, because Jesus our Lord died for us.
Pastor: Christ is the victorious Son of God, who conquered temptation and strengthens us to live a victorious life.
People: We trust in our crucified Lord to give us victory over the power of sin!

Collect
Most holy Father, whose Son Jesus Christ conquered the power of sin for all who put their trust in him: Draw us into your presence, where we may feel your love flood our lives; that Christ's victory over sin and death may give us the victory of renewed living. In his name we pray. Amen.

Prayer of Confession
We admire the cross as our religious symbol, Father; but its message of victory over sin is not as true for us as it ought to be. Forgive us for our satisfaction with being defeated by sin, rather than longing for Christ's power over evil. Rekindle the desire in our hearts for righteousness and Christian living, that Christ's victory over sin may become our victory. We pray in his name. Amen.

Hymns
"All Hail the Power of Jesus' Name"
"Go to Dark Gethsemane"
"In the Cross of Christ I Glory"
"In the Hour of Trial"

SECOND SUNDAY OF LENT

First Lesson: Genesis 17:1-10, 15-19
Theme: God's everlasting covenant

Call to Worship

Pastor: We are blessed by God because he chose to establish a covenant with his people forever.
People: Even as Abraham was blessed by God, so God blesses us with his promises.
Pastor: God's covenant involves two parties. He has given himself to us. Now he asks us to give ourselves to him.
People: We give thanks to God for his covenant, and offer ourselves to him in loyal devotion.

Collect

Loving Father, who commits yourself to your children in a covenant relationship without any proof of their worthiness: Reveal your covenant love to us; that we may turn from our sins and live a new life in faithfulness to your covenant. In Christ's name we pray. Amen.

Prayer of Confession

You are our Father, O God, and we are your children who depend on your goodness. But we often take your presence for granted, unaware of your constant blessings. Forgive us when we sin against your covenant love. Come into our lives, and show us your love; that we may become new persons in Christ Jesus our Lord, through whom we pray. Amen.

Hymns

"Come, Thou Fount of Every Blessing"
"Draw Thou My Soul, O Christ"
"Lord, Jesus I Love Thee"
"More Love to Thee, O Christ"

SECOND SUNDAY OF LENT

Second Lesson: Romans 4:16-25
Theme: The faith of Abraham

Call to Worship

Pastor: Abraham was a godly person because he had complete faith in God's promises.

People: God accepted Abraham as being righteous because he had that kind of faith in God.

Pastor: We, too, can be accepted as righteous, by putting our faith in Jesus, who died for our sins, granting us redemption.

People: What a wonderful salvation God promises through Jesus! He is our Savior in whom we put our faith.

Collect

Father in heaven, who considers righteous those who believe the promises you make: Give us faith like that of Abraham; that we may be accepted as righteous by our faith in Jesus, who promises forgiveness to all who believe. In his name we pray. Amen.

Prayer of Confession

We want to be considered righteous, Father, but our sins are so many. And when we realize how sinful we are, it is difficult to feel we are justified. Forgive us for our many sins, but especially for our weak faith in the promises of Jesus to redeem us. Lead us into an acceptance of salvation, believing we are forgiven, and therefore accepted as righteous by the grace of Jesus, through whom we pray. Amen.

Hymns

"Have Faith in God, My Heart"
"My Hope Is Built"
"Standing on the Promises"
"Tis So Sweet to Trust in Jesus"

SECOND SUNDAY OF LENT

Gospel: Mark 8:31-38
Theme: Only a crucified Christ

Call to Worship
Pastor: Jesus came as Lord, Savior, Son of God. Yet he was destined to die on a cross.
People: The power of sin seems to outweigh the love of God in each generation.
Pastor: It may seem that way. But the cross was necessary to show that God's love in reality is more powerful than man's sin.
People: May we hear the message of the cross speak of Christ crucified on our behalf.

Collect
Most gracious Father, whose love and forgiveness could only be expressed by your Son crucified on our behalf: Move us by your love to accept Jesus as our crucified and risen Lord; that we may walk in newness of life, reborn through faith in his saving grace. In his name we pray. Amen.

Prayer of Confession
We pay high respect to your Son, Father; but we live in disrespect. We cherish the old rugged cross, but give little thought to atonement. We require a crucified Lord to give us the hope of new life. Forgive us for worshiping pride, greatness, and esteem, unaware that they are the reasons for the cross. Help us to come to that cross and find the forgiveness and redemption which you offer. We pray through Christ, our crucified Lord. Amen.

Hymns
"Beneath the Cross of Jesus"
"Cross of Jesus, Cross of Sorrow"
"Must Jesus Bear the Cross Alone"
"When I Survey the Wondrous Cross"

THIRD SUNDAY OF LENT

First Lesson: Exodus 20:1-17
Theme: Rules for our covenant relationship with God

Call to Worship

Pastor: The God who gave deliverance to the Israelites also gave directions on how to live as his children.
People: Our covenant relationship with God is a life in which God is committed to us and we are committed to him.
Pastor: There is only one God. We are to give him our reverence, and respect one another as his children.
People: Praise God for bringing us into his covenant! May we always be faithful in our commitment.

Collect

Almighty God, who has spoken with authority to those who want the blessing of living in a covenant relationship with you: Give us obedient hearts, that we may follow your will, and remain in your covenant. We pray in Jesus' name. Amen.

Prayer of Confession

We know there is a difference between right and wrong, Father. But we want to decide what that difference is when you have already made that decision. Forgive us when we choose our own standards for right living, in denial of your authority to direct us. Help us to be faithful and responsible in living the covenant life to which we have been saved. In Jesus' name we pray. Amen.

Hymns

"Author of Faith, Eternal Word"
"Spirit of God, Descend upon My Heart"
"The Righteous Ones"
"When We Walk with the Lord"

THIRD SUNDAY OF LENT

Second Lesson: 1 Corinthians 1:22-25
Theme: The wisdom of God

Call to Worship
Pastor: The cross has been a stumbling block for many people, because it appears as God's weakness rather than his power.
People: God's wisdom is hard to understand for people who want faith to make sense.
Pastor: The message of the cross is not logical. But it is easy to accept if we believe God loves us in spite of our sins.
People: May God give us new insights into the wisdom of his love!

Collect
Eternal God our Father, whose wisdom far excels our knowledge, and whose power makes our strength as weakness: Give us a clear understanding of the strength and wisdom your love expressed on the cross; that we may experience forgiveness of sin through your Son, Jesus, in whose name we pray. Amen.

Prayer of Confession
Our Father, we lack depth in our faith by not coming to grips with the saving act of Jesus on the cross. We believe he died for our sins; but we learn to say that without knowing the power of your love to save us to a new life. Forgive us when we limit our faith to only that which makes sense to us. Give us faith which lets us trust completely in your power and wisdom to redeem us as your children. We pray in our Savior's name. Amen.

Hymns
"Ask Ye What Great Thing I Know"
"O Love Divine, What Hast Thou Done"
"There Is A Fountain"
"What Wondrous Love Is This"

THIRD SUNDAY OF LENT

Gospel: John 2:13-22
Theme: Jesus cleanses the Temple

Call to Worship

Leader: God communicates with his people through the act of worship, an experience which brings God and humanity together.

People: **We can worship God anywhere. But we share corporately this sanctuary, which we call God's house.**

Leader: When Jesus cleansed the Temple, he demonstrated a cleansing which restores a true relationship between God and his worshipers.

People: **We are in God's house; but more important, we are the body of Christ! May our worship bear witness to who we are.**

Collect

Eternal God, who desires worship to be motivated from a devout heart, not from legal requirements: Cleanse our hearts of all that hinders our communion with you, that we may be honest and sincere in our devotion to you. In our Savior's name we pray. Amen.

Prayer of Confession

We are ashamed on your behalf, Father, of the moneychangers Jesus had to chase from the Temple. Yet in our own day, we abuse your church with false devotion. Christ has built his church of flesh and blood; and we still desecrate that which is consecrated to him. Forgive us for insincere prayers and promises. Inspire us with holiness which will make your church a faithful witness to our Savior, through whom we pray. Amen.

Hymns

"I Want a Principle Within"
"Love Divine, All Loves Excelling"
"O Come, and Dwell in Me"
"O For a Heart to Praise My God"

FOURTH SUNDAY OF LENT

First Lesson: 2 Chronicles 36:14-23
Theme: The Babylonian exile

Call to Worship

Pastor: God is merciful and gracious, willing to forgive; but his justice brings punishment when faith is rejected.

People: Scripture reveals that when we abuse our faith and disobey God's will, God pronounces judgment.

Pastor: Like the Israelites who were exiled for their unfaithfulness, we, too, become captives when faith gives way to sin.

People: Life often seems like exile when we stray from God. May God inspire us with a resurrection of faith and loyalty.

Collect

Almighty God, who punishes those who persist in denying the truths of the faith they profess: Give us receptive hearts to your word of warning; that we may grow in our faith and devotion, giving honor and glory to Christ our Lord, through whom we pray. Amen.

Prayer of Confession

The Babylonian exile fades into the past like a dream, Father, and we feel safe from a God who punishes those who practice faith redesigned by the influence of sin. Forgive us for hardened hearts which make us deaf to your word, and deserters of the faith. Renew us in full surrender to our Savior who died for us. In his name we pray. Amen.

Hymns

"My Faith Looks Up to Thee"
"O For A Faith that Will Not Shrink"
"Pass Me Not, O Gentle Savior"
"Sinners, Turn: Why Will You Die"

FOURTH SUNDAY OF LENT

Second Lesson: Ephesians 2:4-10
Theme: Dead in sin, alive in Christ — by God's grace!

Call to Worship

Pastor: God, in his great mercy, pours out his grace upon us!

People: We are people whose past is sinful. We are people whose nature is sinful. We are people whose life is dead in sin. Yet God makes us alive in Christ!

Pastor: God saves us, not by any righteousness we claim, but only by his benevolent grace.

People: May our lives become fruitful with good deeds in thanksgiving for God's saving grace!

Collect

Most merciful Father, who by grace gives new life to those who are dead in sin: Raise us to new life in Christ; that our lives may give witness to your marvelous grace, freely bestowed through our Savior Jesus Christ, in whose name we pray. Amen.

Prayer of Confession

How often we speak of your grace, Father, for we know we desperately need it. With all our good intentions, our good examples, and our good works, we simply are sinners who have no hope except for your grace. Forgive us for our sinful desires and shameful behavior which destroy our lives. Stir our hearts with your love; that we may receive your grace, and become new persons in Christ, through whom we pray. Amen.

Hymns

"Alas! and Did My Savior Bleed"
"Amazing Grace"
"Beneath the Cross of Jesus"
"Depth of Mercy"

FOURTH SUNDAY OF LENT

Gospel: John 3:14-21
Theme: God loves the world

Call to Worship

Leader: The cross, once a symbol of death, has become a symbol of life for the Christian.
People: **It was on the cross that Jesus was lifted up in atonement for our sins.**
Leader: God has demonstrated the depth of his love through his only Son, that, believing in him, we may have eternal life.
People: **We believe Jesus died on our behalf, saving us from the guilt of sin, and giving us the gift of eternal life.**

Collect

O God our heavenly Father, whose love for mankind is so intense that you gave your only Son to die on our behalf: Grant us the faith to believe his death on the cross atones for our sins, that we may know your gift of eternal life is ours. In our Redeemer's name we pray. Amen.

Prayer of Confession

You love us dearly, Father, yet how indifferent we are! We take your love for granted without considering the price you have paid, or the blessing you give when your love is accepted. Forgive us for requiring such depth of love, and then not responding with our faith and trust. Fill our hearts, our minds, and our lives, with belief in your Son as our crucified Savior, that we may receive the eternal blessing of your love. In his name we pray. Amen.

Hymns

"Alas! and Did My Savior Bleed"
"O Love Divine, That Stooped to Share"
"O Love Divine, What Hast Thou Done"
"Savior, Thy Dying Love"

FIFTH SUNDAY OF LENT

First Lesson: Jeremiah 31:31-34
Theme: The new covenant written in our hearts

Call to Worship

Pastor: The cross speaks of the new covenant which God had promised through his prophet Jeremiah.
People: It is a covenant written in our hearts instead of on tablets of stone.
Pastor: It is a covenant with God, sealed by the blood of Christ who died on the cross for our sins.
People: It is a new covenant in which we accept God's love and commit our lives to him.

Collect

Almighty God, who promised a new covenant with your children, and who established that covenant through the death of your only Son: Impress your love within our hearts; that we may respond with devotion, in the knowledge that you have redeemed us through the blood of your Son, our Savior, in whose name we pray. Amen.

Prayer of Confession

Dear Father, your laws are eternal truths which we believe, but which we confine to our Bibles. Even with your new covenant, we harden our hearts for fear you may gain more control of our lives than we desire. Forgive us for our resistance to your love expressed in this new covenant sealed by the blood of Jesus your Son. Pour your spirit into our hearts, that we may know the joy of living in this new covenant relationship. We pray in our Savior's name. Amen.

Hymns

"Come, Thou Fount"
"I Am Coming to the Cross"
"Jesus, Keep Me Near the Cross"
"O For A Heart to Praise My God"

FIFTH SUNDAY OF LENT

Second Lesson: Hebrews 5:7-10
Theme: Jesus, obedient to death, intercedes for us

Call to Worship
Pastor: God is able to bring us into his covenant love because Jesus was obedient even in suffering.
People: Jesus suffered death for us because he was willing to be used by God to establish a new covenant with his people.
Pastor: Through death, Jesus became the source of our salvation, interceding with God on our behalf.
People: May Christ's obedience to death inspire us to obedient living, in thanksgiving for our salvation!

Collect
Eternal God, whose Son was obedient to your will, suffering even death to save us in a new covenant relationship with you: Give us the desire and the fortitude to be obedient followers, that we may receive the salvation which Christ's death mediates. In his name we pray. Amen.

Prayer of Confession
We are moved by the intense struggle of Jesus, who suffered not for his own sin, Father, but for ours. His obedience, which brought him death, brings us life. Forgive us for our sins of disobedience and rejection which make Jesus' obedience to death necessary for our restoration to life. Restore us in your new covenant; that we may be bound to you by our Savior's love, in whose name we pray. Amen.

Hymns
"Alone Thou Goest Forth"
"Go to Dark Gethsemane"
"I Stand Amazed in the Presence"
" 'Tis Midnight, and on Olive's Brow"

FIFTH SUNDAY OF LENT

Gospel: John 12:20-33
Theme: Christ's death gives life to all who believe

Call to Worship

Leader: We find Jesus only when we approach him as one who died on the cross for our sins.
People: As a single grain must die to produce life in many other grains, so Jesus' death gives life to all who follow him.
Leader: Our crucified Lord draws us to himself, that we may be restored to fellowship with God our Father.
People: We see Jesus lifted up in death for us, giving us new life with God our Father!

Collect

Gracious God, who gave your Son a victorious death upon the cross, giving life to all who look to him: Direct us through our sinful existence to see his death as our source of salvation, that we may experience the new life for which he died. In his name we pray. Amen.

Prayer of Confession

Hear our confession of sin, O God, and grant us forgiveness for the sake of Christ who died on the cross for us. We come as seekers, desiring new life and release from our guilt, believing that Jesus, lifted upon the cross, has drawn us into his presence where we are revived by your love. With the breath of your Spirit, breathe new life into our souls, that we may walk in newness of life now and forever. In Jesus' name we pray. Amen.

Hymns

"Beneath the Cross of Jesus"
"Breathe on Me, Breath of God"
"O Sacred Head, Now Wounded"
"When I Survey the Wondrous Cross"

SIXTH SUNDAY OF LENT
(When observed as Passion Sunday)

First Lesson: Isaiah 50:4-9a
Theme: Discipleship requires commitment

Call to Worship
Pastor: Jesus illustrated with his life that obedience to God is not a life of ease and pleasure.
People: Discipleship requires disciplined commitment in our Lord's service.
Pastor: Christ is our example who was faithful even to death.
People: We know God preserves those who are faithful to him. We pray for courage to be faithful.

Collect
Father in heaven, who defends those who are faithful in their discipleship: Give us courage in the face of criticism and opposition; that we may be loyal in our service to Christ, through whom we pray. Amen.

Prayer of Confession
Forgive us, Father, when we try to be disciples without disciplined obedience. Forgive us when we try to be followers of Christ only until he leads us into conflict. Forgive us when we try to be faithful without courage to face the faithless. Give us a commitment to Christ which will keep us loyal in all forms of Christian service. In Christ's name we pray. Amen.

Hymns
"He Who Would Valiant Be"
"O Jesus, I Have Promised"
"Stand Up, Stand Up for Jesus"
"When We Walk with the Lord"

SIXTH SUNDAY OF LENT
(When observed as Passion Sunday)

Second Lesson: Philippians 2:5-11
Theme: Christ's obedience to death

Call to Worship
Pastor: We worship Jesus, who had the nature of God, but took the nature of a servant.
People: He humbly walked the path of obedience, even to death.
Pastor: For this reason, Christ who suffered death for us, God has exalted above all in heaven and on earth.
People: Jesus Christ is Lord! Praise his glorious name!

Collect
Father in heaven, whose Son obediently followed his servant role even to the cross on our behalf: Take our wills and remold us into your servants; that like Christ, we too, may find the joy of serving you. In his name we pray. Amen.

Prayer of Confession
May all the world fall on their knees and worship Jesus as King! How much we want that, Father, and yet we must confess, that our hearts have not always kept pace with our lips. Forgive us when we fail in our discipleship to be obedient servants of Christ. Reaffirm us in our faith; that we may give true praise and devotion to Christ, the King of our lives, through whom we pray. Amen.

Hymns
"All Praise to Thee, for Thou, O King Divine"
"Crown Him with Many Crowns"
"Ride On, Ride On in Majesty"
"The Son of God Goes Forth to War"

SIXTH SUNDAY OF LENT
(When observed as Passion Sunday)

Gospel: Mark 14:1—15:47 or 15:1-39
Theme: Jesus is the suffering, but triumphant King

Call to Worship
Pastor: Jesus rode into Jerusalem in triumph, but his real triumph was accomplished on the cross.
People: **Jesus triumphed because he was willing to take the way of the cross. Only then could he defeat the power of sin and death.**
Pastor: Evil always seems more powerful, but our Lord demonstrated his power once and for all. Now he is King, and desires to rule in every heart.
People: **What mighty acts God performs for his children! We praise him for his Son, Jesus, Ruler of our lives!**

Collect
Heavenly Father, who led your Son to the cross, that sinners may experience the power of your love: Take us to the cross, that we may experience Christ's victory in atonement for our sins, and give witness to that experience with our praise. In his name we pray. Amen.

Prayer of Confession
Palm branches, once held high in praise, lay crumpled on the dusty road, Father. And Jesus went to Calvary. How often our empty praises fall like broken palms, unsupported by dedication or discipleship. We, too, send our Lord to Calvary. Forgive us for our sins which require a crucified Lord. Come into our lives with the victory of forgiveness and new life; that we may become living disciples of our living Lord, in whose name we pray. Amen.

Hymns
"All Glory, Laud, And Honor"
"Behold the Savior of Mankind"
"Lift Up Your Heads, Ye Mighty Gates"
"Ride On, Ride On in Majesty"

SIXTH SUNDAY OF LENT
(When observed as Palm Sunday)

First Lesson: Isaiah 50:4-9, (Psalm 118:19-29)
Theme: Praise to Christ, the King

Call to Worship
Pastor: Some would shout praise, and others curses. Some would swing branches, and others, whips.
People: **Christ, the Son of God! Some would claim him King, and others, a heretic.**
Pastor: Where are we in the crowds of each generation? Do our lips and lives agree?
People: **With hearts, and hands, and voices, we unite to magnify Christ, the King of our lives!**

Collect
Eternal God, who not only sent your Son to save us, but strengthened him for his ministry of reconciliation: Let the praise of our lips this day, reflect the life we intend to live; that we may be faithful followers of your Son all our days. In his name we pray. Amen.

Prayer of Confession
Forgive us, Father, when we have contributed to the pain our Lord endured instead of giving him the praise he deserves. Lead us in our commitment to give faithful service and honest witness; that our participation in the ongoing history of the church may encourage followers rather than discourage them. In our Savior's name we pray. Amen.

Hymns
"Lead On, O King Eternal"
"Lift Up Your Heads, Ye Mighty Gates"
"O Worship the King"
"Ride On, Ride On in Majesty"

SIXTH SUNDAY OF LENT
(When observed as Palm Sunday)

Second Lesson: Philippians 2:5-11
Theme: The obedient Christ is exalted by God

Call to Worship
Pastor: Hail to Christ the King! He gave up the nature of God to assume the nature of a servant.
People: In humility and obedience, Jesus accepted death on the cross to give us a glorious life.
Pastor: Therefore God has exalted him with blessing and honor, that all beings in heaven and earth should bow down and worship him.
People: Glory be to God our Father, who has made Jesus Christ Lord of our lives!

Collect
Heavenly Father, whose Son gave up his heavenly nature to suffer the abuse of humanity, defeating sin for all who believe in him: Let the praise of our lips come from sincere hearts, that we may surrender our lives to his rule and redemption. In his name we pray. Amen.

Prayer of Confession
We have praised your Son with our lips, Father; but we fear that our songs of praise will fade away when we are left to face our true feelings. Our lips are conditioned for praise today, but our hearts are conditioned for disobedience. Forgive us for saying what we do not feel, and feeling what we ought not say. Put real joy in our hearts; that we may be sincere in our praise of your Son, our Savior, through whom we pray. Amen.

Hymns
"All Hail the Power of Jesus' Name"
"All Praise to Thee, for Thou, O King Divine"
"At the Name of Jesus"
"Rejoice the Lord Is King"

SIXTH SUNDAY OF LENT
(When observed as Palm Sunday)

Gospel: Mark 11:1-11 or John 12:12-16
Theme: The Triumphant entry

Call to Worship

Leader [Pastor:] When Jesus rode into Jerusalem on the donkey, he was a living fulfillment of the promised King.

People: **His Kingdom is without end. We, too, hail him as our King, and pledge him our allegiance.**

Leader [Pastor:] We are part of a mighty church that spans the centuries, called to proclaim our Lord's Kingship to all people.

People: **May we take up the banner and wave it proudly; that our generation may know who Jesus is.**

Collect

Almighty God, you have given your Son full authority over our lives. Give us submissive wills to yield to his authority; that we may enjoy the blessings of living in your kingdom. In the name of Christ we pray. Amen.

Prayer of Confession

We are repeating that Palm Sunday of long ago, Father, and hail your Son as our King. But we, like those before us, have selfish reasons for wanting a king. Forgive us when we misunderstand the kingship of Christ without giving our allegiance. Give your Son victory in our lives; that we may follow in the way he leads, and share in his kingdom. In his name we pray. Amen.

Hymns

"All Glory, Laud and Honor"
"Hosanna, Loud Hosanna"
"Lift Up Your Heads, Ye Mighty Gates"
"Ride On, Ride On in Majesty"

MONDAY IN HOLY WEEK

First Lesson: Isaiah 42:1-9
Theme: First Servant Song: a Spirit-filled Servant

Call to Worship

Pastor: God has sent his Servant, and has filled him with his Spirit to make right the wrongs of our world.

People: We worship Jesus who came as God's Servant with the healing ministry which God promised to his Servant.

Pastor: Through Jesus, God delivers us from our prisons of sin, and brings us into a new covenant with him.

People: God's light has pierced the darkness of our sin with the love of Jesus. Praise God for our deliverance!

Collect

Eternal God, who filled your Son, Jesus, with your Holy Spirit, entrusting him with a mission of justice and deliverance for the oppressed: Let his ministry reach into our lives with healing and wholeness; that we may be freed from sin to live in the new covenant, sealed by Christ our Savior, in whose name we pray. Amen.

Prayer of Confession

We read from the Old Testament of your Servant, O God, whom you promised to fill with your Spirit. From the New Testament we read of your Son who fulfills that promise. But we look at ourselves today, and we feel the power of sin destroying the life we want to live. Deliver us from our bondage to sin with the love and forgiveness of your Son. Come into the darkness of our hearts, that we may be delivered into the light of your love. In our Savior's name we pray. Amen.

Hymns

"Come, Ye Disconsolate"
"Come, Ye Sinners, Poor and Needy"
"I Heard the Voice of Jesus Say"
"Thou Hidden Source of Calm Repose"

MONDAY IN HOLY WEEK

Second Lesson: Hebrews 9:11-15
Theme: Christ's sacrifice continues to be redemptive

Call to Worship

Pastor: We have been brought into a new covenant relationship with God through Jesus Christ.

People: In death, Jesus became a perfect sacrifice for the sins of the whole world.

Pastor: This new covenant is sealed by Jesus' blood which atones for the sins of all who believe in him.

People: We claim salvation through Christ, whose sacrifice brings us into a new covenant with God.

Collect

Eternal God, whose Son takes away the guilt of sin for all who believe in him, by his one perfect sacrifice on the cross: Accept us in your new covenant, cleansed by his blood, that we may receive your promised blessings, and serve you faithfully all our days. We pray through Christ our Lord. Amen.

Prayer of Confession

We feel the guilt of sin, Father, and know that we separate ourselves from you. In various ways we try to give sacrificial offerings to make up for our sins, but still we are not relieved of our guilt. Forgive us through Christ's death on the cross. Convince us of his cleansing which continues to save sinners through his shed blood, that we may be inspired to live as children of your covenant. In our Savior's name we pray. Amen.

Hymns

"Alas! and Did My Saviour Bleed"
"Come, Thou Fount of Every Blessing"
"Jesus, Thy Blood and Righteousness"
"There Is a Fountain Filled with Blood"

MONDAY IN HOLY WEEK

Gospel: John 12:1-11
Theme: Mary anoints Jesus with expensive perfume

Call to Worship
Pastor: Today, we know the presence of Jesus through his Spirit. Think what it must have been to be with him in person!
People: Some appreciated being with Jesus so much, they could not bear the thought of his death.
Pastor: Nevertheless Jesus could not always be with his followers in body. Only through his death could he become the resurrection and the life.
People: His love demands our all. May our devotion be free of selfish interest and worldly concern.

Collect
O loving Father, who gave your Son a limited earthly ministry so that he could minister to our spiritual needs forever: Move us to sincere devotion, that our commitment to Christ may be without concern for the material worth of our affection. In his name we pray. Amen.

Prayer of Confession
We are too careful, Father, of how we express our love to you. But when we spend love on ourselves, we know no limits. Forgive us when we carefully discipline ourselves from extravagant expressions of devotion. Release us from the worship of wealth and the god of greed, that we may be free to love you as disciples of Christ our Lord, in whose name we pray. Amen.

Hymns
"Alone Thou Goest Forth"
"O Thou, in Whose Presence"
"What Shall I Do My God to Love"
"When I Survey the Wondrous Cross"

TUESDAY IN HOLY WEEK

First Lesson: Isaiah 49:1-7
Theme: Second Servant Song: a universal mission

Call to Worship

Pastor: God's people are all the people of the world. And one thing we have in common is sin.

People: We are indeed lost together, because we all agree to sin against our God.

Pastor: But God has sent his Son to be his Servant, bringing forgiveness through his death on the cross to all who believe in him.

People: We join with all Christians to praise our Lord for his salvation!

Collect

Most gracious Father, whose love reaches out to all people, through the saving act of your Son and through your church which continues his ministry: Make us effective in your service, that we may represent our Lord with his gift of salvation for all people. In his name we pray. Amen.

Prayer of Confession

Father, we have been with those who despise righteousness and reject salvation. Even when we want to be righteous, we decide what makes righteousness righteous. And then we are like the Pharisees who crucified your Son. Forgive us for our resistance to follow in your paths. Grant us your light which reveals our sin and your salvation. Then send us to share that light with our world; that all may have the opportunity to know redemption through your Son, in whose name we pray. Amen.

Hymns

"Ah, Holy Jesus"
"Break Forth, O Living Light of God"
"Christ Is the World's True Light"
"Walk in the Light"

TUESDAY IN HOLY WEEK

Second Lesson: 1 Corinthians 1:18-31
Theme: Self-righteous wisdom conflicts with the cross

Call to Worship
Pastor: Religious knowledge is not the means of a right relationship with God.
People: God communicates with our hearts, more than our heads, when he invites us into salvation.
Pastor: The cross of Christ is our way to salvation. We cannot bypass that, even with all the religious wisdom of the world.
People: God's love is beyond human understanding. But by faith, we accept it and believe in Christ our Savior.

Collect
Almighty God, whose wisdom has found a way to save the unsavable: Deliver us from our burden of sin through the grace of Christ, that we may feel in our hearts the salvation which we believe our Savior's death on the cross makes possible. In his name we pray. Amen.

Prayer of Confession
We become what we think in our hearts, Father, but what we think in our minds often confuses the meditation of our hearts. And so we learn to doubt, or argue, resulting in religious dialogue without spiritual cleansing. Forgive us when we have valued self-righteous wisdom more than lives changed by the love of Christ. Lead us to the cross where we may feel our lives transformed by our Savior, that our faith may grow through experience rather than reason. Hear us for Christ's sake. Amen.

Hymns
"Beneath the Cross of Jesus"
"In the Cross of Christ I Glory"
"Jesus, Keep Me Near the Cross"
"When I Survey the Wondrous Cross"

TUESDAY IN HOLY WEEK

Gospel: John 12:20-36
Theme: Servants of the Servant

Call to Worship
Pastor: Faith is a gift from God to those who will accept it. But it requires the giving of ourselves in trust to God.
People: God inspires us to believe in him, and enables us to put our trust in him. That is the faith which God gives.
Pastor: When God promises, we believe. When God leads we follow. That is the response faith stirs in us.
People: May God's revelation in Christ stir us to faith in his salvation, and obedience to his leading.

Collect
Father in heaven, whose Son gave his life as a Servant, and called us into his service: Strengthen our faith and commitment; that we may follow Jesus not only as Savior, but also as Lord. In his name we pray. Amen.

Prayer of Confession
Father, we are believers in name, but not always followers in practice. Forgive us when our faith wavers, keeping us from following Christ as loyal servants. Bring us into firm discipleship; that we may be builders of Christ's church, with a strong witness for Jesus our Savior, in whose name we pray. Amen.

Hymns
"Am I a Soldier of the Cross"
"Holy Spirit, Faithful Guide"
"In the Hour of Trial"
"O For a Faith that Will Not Shrink"

WEDNESDAY IN HOLY WEEK

First Lesson: Isaiah 50:4-9a
Theme: Third Servant Song: obedience in suffering

Call to Worship
Pastor: Jesus was God's obedient Servant, even when he suffered the abuse of those he wanted to save.
People: Jesus knew who he was, and he knew his mission. He also knew God would help him endure.
Pastor: He knew sinners could be saved, and loved them to that end.
People: We know God loves us, because Jesus was obedient to death on the cross. By his death, we sinners are made alive!

Collect
Father of mercy, whose Son went to the cross to save sinners even though rejected by them: Forgive the insults our lives have brought to your Son, that our lives may now give praise and thanksgiving for the salvation he has brought to us. In Christ's name we pray. Amen.

Prayer of Confession
Our Father, your Son walks among us in Spirit. And our lives, which we think are good and acceptable, insult him with dishonor. Yet, with patience and love, he continues to offer salvation. Forgive us for our sins of selfrighteousness, of self-esteem, of apathy, of false devotion. Let his presence move us to conviction of sin and commitment to discipleship, that our witness may support, rather than hinder, his ministry today. In our Savior's name we pray. Amen.

Hymns
"Behold the Savior of Mankind"
"Cross of Jesus, Cross of Sorrow"
"O Love Divine, What Hast Thou Done"
"What Wondrous Love Is This"

WEDNESDAY IN HOLY WEEK

Second Lesson: Hebrews 12:1-3
Theme: Encouraged by Christ's victory

Call to Worship

Pastor: We share in a fellowship of God's people which bridges the centuries from the beginning of time.
People: We are encouraged by the many saints who have gone before us, who were faithful in their generation.
Pastor: Christ himself is our chief example. He did not give up, even when faced with the cross.
People: We are confident, with Christ's help, that we, too, will be victorious over the struggles of this life.

Collect

Heavenly Father, whose Son accepted the shame of the cross that we might enjoy the blessing of your love: Give us the courage to be faithful in our discipleship; that his death may not have been in vain. In his name we pray. Amen.

Prayer of Confession

Father, we marvel at the faith of so many who did not give up under severe persecution. And yet we, who are not really persecuted, can be so weak in our convictions when tested. Forgive us when we seem so unsure of the faith we profess. Strengthen us for committed living that will keep us true to the Christ we love, in whose name we pray. Amen.

Hymns

"Beneath the Cross of Jesus"
"Dear Master, in Whose Life I See"
"Go to Dark Gethsemane"
"Must Jesus Bear the Cross Alone"

WEDNESDAY IN HOLY WEEK

Gospel: John 13:21-30
Theme: Judas becomes the traitor

Call to Worship
Pastor: The rejection of Jesus is personified in one person: Judas.
People: Judas represents the ugliness of the human race, because even though he was a close companion of Jesus, he betrayed him for personal gain.
Pastor: We know that evil is in all of us and do not want it to get out of hand.
People: We know that temptation; but we trust God to lead us by his Spirit in a life of full commitment.

Collect
Almighty God, whose Son was misunderstood and abused by a traitor's greed: Reaffirm us in the Christian faith to be steadfast in our loyalty, that we may never let our sins interfere with your desire to redeem us. In our Savior's name we pray. Amen.

Prayer of Confession
We wonder, Father, how often our acknowledgment of Christ has brought more hurt than help. We are professing Christians, yet much of our testimony becomes superficial like a betrayer's kiss. Forgive us for any companionship with Christ which demonstrates a selfish relationship. Convict us of our false allegiance, that we may surrender ourselves in true devotion out of sincere love. We pray in Jesus' name. Amen.

Hymns
"Go to Dark Gethsemane"
"In the Hour of Trial"
"O Jesus, I Have Promised"
"'Tis Midnight, and on Olive's Brow"

THURSDAY IN HOLY WEEK
(Maundy Thursday)

First Lesson: Exodus 24:3-8
Theme: Remember and celebrate

Call to Worship
Pastor: We cannot look at the Lord's Table without looking at his cross.
People: We come to the Table, and remember the price our Savior paid on the cross to redeem us from sin.
Pastor: We celebrate our deliverance from sin as we commune in memory of our Lord who died for us.
People: Christ cleanses us from sin! We celebrate with thanksgiving his cleansing love!

Collect
Gracious Father, whose Son has directed his followers to remember his Last Supper in celebration of deliverance from sin: Remind us of the great price our Lord paid to deliver us from sin, that we may celebrate with honest joy the new life to which we have been delivered. In his name we pray. Amen.

Prayer of Confession
We bow before you in humility and in penitence, Father, confessing that we have sinned against your love. As we call to mind the great sacrifice of your Son, cause us also to remember our sins which make his sacrifice necessary for us. Forgive us for our sins; that our remembrance will stir us to celebrate with praise, our new life in Christ Jesus our Lord, through whom we pray. Amen.

Hymns
"According to Thy Gracious Word"
"Come, Sinners, to the Gospel Feast"
"In Memory of the Savior's Love"
"Jesus, Keep Me Near the Cross"

THURSDAY IN HOLY WEEK
(Maundy Thursday)

Second Lesson: 1 Corinthians 10:16-21
Theme: A communion of Christians with Christ

Call to Worship

Leader: We come to our Lord's Table in celebration of our Savior's love which redeems us from sin.
People: As we eat the bread and drink the cup, we share in the body and blood of Christ.
Leader: We are one with Christ, united in a communion which strengthens our allegiance to him.
People: We will eat and drink in witness of our unity with Christ our Savior, and identify ourselves as his disciples.

Collect

Almighty Father, whose Son is one with us as we eat and drink in celebration of his sacrifice for our sins: Make the witness of our participation true, as we come to your table, that our communion may be with our hearts more than our lips. We pray through Christ our Lord. Amen.

Prayer of Confession

We come to your table, Father, to commune with our Savior. We eat the bread, because his body was broken to make us whole. We drink the cup, because his blood was shed for our sins. Have mercy upon us, and forgive our sins for which our Savior suffered. Commune with us in this Sacrament, that our participation may strengthen us to be disciples who live by the faith we profess. In our Savior's name we pray. Amen.

Hymns

"Be Known to Us in Breaking Bread"
"Here, O My Lord, I See Thee"
"How Happy Are Thy Servants, Lord"
"Spirit of God, Descend upon My Heart"

THURSDAY IN HOLY WEEK
(Maundy Thursday)

Gospel: Mark 14:12-26
Theme: Forgiveness for betrayers

Call to Worship

Pastor: [Leader] Our Lord has invited us to commune with him, even though we are guilty of betraying him.
People: We would not "sell" our Lord. Yet we have betrayed him for less than silver.
Pastor: [Leader] Our Lord knows what we have done. But he still invites us to his table in hope that, unlike Judas, we will accept God's forgiveness.
People: We come in confession of our guilt, and in acceptance of the forgiveness our Lord offers.

Collect

O loving Father, who forgives even those who betray your love: Assure us of your forgiveness for our behavior which betrays your love; that as we commune, we may give ourselves back to you in a new love relationship, ~~strong enough to overcome any further betrayal. In our Savior's name we pray.~~ Amen.

Prayer of Confession

Forgive us, Father, for we have betrayed your sacred gift of love. For the price of enjoyment in sinful pleasures, material gains to satisfy our greed, and acceptance by our friends, we have denied our allegiance to you. We are unworthy of your love, but we confess we cannot live without it. Receive us back into discipleship as we come to your table this evening. We pray through your Son, our Savior, who shed his blood for us. Amen.

Hymns

"Alas! and Did My Savior Bleed"
"Come, Every Soul by Sin Oppressed"
"Come, Sinners, to the Gospel Feast"
"In Memory of the Savior's Love"

GOOD FRIDAY

First Lesson: Isaiah 52:13 — 53:12
Theme: Jesus assumes sin's disgrace

Call to Worship

Pastor: Sin is the prelude to defeat. It nourishes disgrace, and produces shame.
People: The glory with which sin allures us is false and short lived. It leads to self-destruction.
Pastor: But Jesus assumed our defeat, that we may be restored as children of God.
People: The love of God is beyond description! Because of us, and yet for us, Jesus died on the cross!

Collect

Gracious Father, whose Son took upon himself the burden and disgrace of our sin: Lift us out of our misery as prisoners of sin; that we may give you praise for our salvation achieved by the death of your Son, Jesus, in whose name we pray. Amen.

Prayer of Confession

We fool ourselves so easily, Father, pretending to be content with the condition of our souls. But deep within, we cry out in anguish, destroyed by the conquest of sin. Forgive us for the dishonor which we have brought, not only to ourselves, but to your Son who suffered because of our sin. Give us the assurance of your love, that we may gain the victory for which our Lord died. In his name we pray. Amen.

Hymns

"Alone Thou Goest Forth"
"O Love Divine, What Hast Thou Done"
"What Wondrous Love Is This"
"When I Survey the Wondrous Cross"

GOOD FRIDAY

Second Lesson: Hebrews 4:14-16, 5:7-9
Theme: Jesus, the perfect high priest

Call to Worship
Pastor: Come to the throne of God, confident that God's mercy and grace are available to you.
People: We come confidently, only because Christ, through his suffering and death, has gone before us.
Pastor: He is our source of salvation, interceding on our behalf, bringing us into reconciliation with God.
People: We honor the day Christ died; for in his death, he brings new life to us with God our Father.

Collect
Most gracious and merciful Father, whose Son is our source of salvation for all who obey him: Grant us courage and steadfastness in our faith; that your mercy and grace may bear fruit in our lives, and bring honor and glory to you. In our Savior's name we pray. Amen.

Prayer of Confession
Today we are thinking of others, Father. Others who misunderstand your Son, and crucified him. Yet even today, we still understand him, when we yield to our sinful ways in denial of his salvation. Forgive us when we act with indifference toward the price our Lord paid for our salvation. Help us to live obediently in thanksgiving for the new life he offers. In his name we pray. Amen.

Hymns
"Alas! and Did My Savior Bleed"
"Majestic Sweetness Sets Enthroned"
"Savior, Thy Dying Love"
"There Is a Fountain Filled with Blood"

GOOD FRIDAY

Gospel: John 18:1—19:42 or John 19:17-30
Theme: Jesus insulted and crucified

Call to Worship

Pastor: Look at the cross and listen. [**Pause**] What do you hear in the silence?
People: The silence echoes like thunder in judgment of our humanity. For we hear the cry of death, of grief, of shame, or guilt.
Pastor: Listen again. Can you hear God speaking above the storm stirred up by sin?
People: Yes! It is as though God is calling us to Calvary to share his forgiveness with us!

Collect

Almighty God, who transformed Calvary's sinful tragedy into a drama of redemption: Speak clearly your word of forgiveness; that our sins may be destroyed, enabling us to live a new life in the service of our Savior, in whose name we pray. Amen.

Prayer of Confession

We have been to Calvary before, Father, just like those who nailed Jesus to the cross. Without hammer, and without nails, we have put Jesus on the cross. All it took was sin. Bring us back to Calvary, Father, this time to experience forgiveness through our crucified Lord. Restore us in love; that we may lead others in their return to Calvary for cleansing. In our Savior's name we pray. Amen.

Hymns

"Beneath the Cross of Jesus"
"In the Cross of Christ I Glory"
"Jesus, Keep Me Near the Cross"
"King of My Life"

EASTER DAY

First Lesson: Isaiah 25:6-9
Theme: God has victory over death

Call to Worship
Pastor: Lift up your hearts, and rejoice in God's victory over death!
People: God has done a mighty work in Jesus, whom he raised from the grave! Praise his glorious name!
Pastor: We are a saved people because God has demonstrated his love and power in Jesus' resurrection!
People: Our joy is without limits, because God has rescued us from the death of sin! Our trust is in Jesus our risen Lord!

Collect
O wonderful God, our Father, who has blessed us with joy and happiness by raising your Son, Jesus, from the grave: Keep us ever mindful of the joy which is forever ours because of Jesus' resurrection; that we may never cease to sing your praises, both with our lips and with our lives. We pray through Christ, our risen Lord. Amen.

Prayer of Confession
We celebrate Christ's resurrection every Sunday, Father. But we tend to concentrate more on our church, than on why we gather together. We are reminded today that you have come to our rescue with love and power to conquer sin and death. Forgive us when we celebrate without joy, the gift of life you have given us through your Son, Jesus, in whose name we pray. Amen.

Hymns
"Christ the Lord Is Risen Today"
"Good Christian Men, Rejoice"
"Jesus Christ Is Risen Today"
"O Sons and Daughters, Let Us Sing"

EASTER DAY

Second Lesson: 1 Corinthians 15:1-11
Theme: The truth of the resurrection

Call to Worship

Pastor: Glory be to God on high! Christ our Lord is risen from the dead!

People: Hallelujah! Not only is Christ risen from the dead; but we too, shall be raised to new life because of him!

Pastor: Yes! We have identified with Adam and his sinful nature. Now we can identify with Christ, and enjoy eternal life.

People: We worship our risen Lord who lives within our hearts!

Collect

Eternal God, our Father, who has reached down to man in our sinful nature with the gift of eternal life through your Son Jesus, our Lord: Raise us to new life, that, turning from our sinfulness, we may enjoy the blessings of resurrection living, now and forever more. We pray through Christ the Resurrection and the life. Amen.

Prayer of Confession

Dear Lord, we thank you for the message of Christ's Resurrection and ours. But we confess, even with our knowledge of the resurrection hope, we still drift so easily into the sinful nature of Adam. Forgive us for not committing ourselves to the reality of our resurrection that Christ has proven to us. We have been united with Adam too long; now, and forever, unite us with Christ our risen Savior, in whose name we pray. Amen.

Hymns

"I Know that My Redeemer Lives"
"Sing with All the Sons of Glory"
"Now the Green Blade Riseth"
"The Strife Is O'er, The Battle Done"

EASTER DAY

Gospel: Mark 16:1-8 or John 20:1-18
Theme: Christ's resurrection

Call to Worship

Leader: The joy of Easter brings us together in worship to celebrate the resurrection of Christ.
People: We worship with the expectation that our faith will be strengthened.
Leader: Our worship will also challenge us to respond with deeper commitment to our risen Lord.
People: We worship our risen Lord, inspired to serve him with renewed discipleship.

Collect

Eternal God, who revealed your victory over the grave through the resurrection of your Son, Jesus: Give us victory over all which destroys the fullness of life you have given us; that we may come alive with renewed faith, in the sure hope that we shall experience fullness of life forever in the presence of Christ our risen Lord, through whom we pray. Amen.

Prayer of Confession

Our search for life has brought us to Christ, Father; but, like his disciples, we misunderstand his ministry and message. We deny ourselves the joy of Christ's presence in our lives as Lord and Savior. Forgive us for letting our discipleship be plagued with disinterest, and our life be threatened by death. Restore us to faithfulness, and raise us to new life, that we may experience a resurrection to eternal fellowship with our Savior, Jesus Christ, in whose name we pray. Amen.

Hymns

"I Know That My Redeemer Lives"
"I Serve a Risen Savior"
"Sing with All the Sons of Glory"
"The Day of Resurrection"

SECOND SUNDAY OF EASTER

First Lesson: Acts 4:32-35
Theme: United in a living witness of Christ's resurrection

Call to Worship

Pastor: Christ's resurrection was a transforming power in the early church, binding them together in love.
People: United in heart and mind, they witnessed to the resurrection with great enthusiasm.
Pastor: God richly blessed them not only in spirit, but fulfilled their needs as they shared all things in common.
People: May our risen Lord unite us in a living witness to the power of his resurrection.

Collect

Gracious Father, who unites your children in love and fellowship by the presence of your risen Son, Jesus: Bless your church with a united faith; that we may give a powerful witness to our world of the rich blessings you give through our risen Lord, in whose name we pray. Amen.

Prayer of Confession

We are thrilled with the presence of our risen Lord, O God, and praise you for his resurrection. But we confess that our enthusiasm is more our personal expression of praise to you, than a united witness to our world. Forgive us when we do not let our risen Lord unite us as a fellowship of believers who share a common faith. Give us a strong witness which reveals the risen Christ in our midst, that we may experience the joy of your rich blessings. In our Savior's name we pray. Amen.

Hymns

"All Praise to Our Redeeming Lord"
"Blest Be the Tie That Binds"
"Jesus, Lord, We Look to Thee"
"Jesus, United by Thy Grace"

SECOND SUNDAY OF EASTER

Second Lesson: 1 John 1:1 — 2:2
Theme: Jesus pleads on our behalf

Call to Worship
Pastor: We love God; but even though we love him, we still sin.
People: Our human nature seems more than we can conquer, in spite of our righteous intentions.
Pastor: If we were perfect, we would not need Jesus to plead on our behalf. But he knows our limitations and intercedes for us.
People: We desire to follow God's commands, but we depend on Christ to cleanse our unrighteousness.

Collect
Most merciful Father, whose Son makes perfect our imperfections by his saving act on the cross: Receive us as children who desire your forgiveness; that we may be enabled to live in union with you through our Lord Jesus Christ, in whose name we pray. Amen.

Prayer of Confession
We feel that we know you, Father; but our lives do not reflect the obedience which such knowledge ought to produce. We have put more in our minds than we are able to give from our hearts. Forgive us when we assume our righteousness so controls us that we no longer need our Lord's help. Keep us mindful of the constant threat of sin; that we may strive for obedience, and then humble ourselves to let our Lord intercede on our behalf. In his name we pray. Amen.

Hymns
"Hail, Thou Once-Despised Jesus"
"Jesus, Thy Blood and Righteousness"
"Just as I Am, Without One Plea"
"When We Walk with the Lord"

SECOND SUNDAY OF EASTER

Gospel: John 20:19-31
Theme: The blessing of faith without sight

Call to Worship

Leader: The resurrection of Christ was an act of God which illustrates victory over sin for every generation.

People: **We are just as thrilled today as those who were blessed with a firsthand experience of Christ's resurrection.**

Leader: We, too, have our firsthand experience because God gives us faith which is more blessed than sight.

People: **We thank God for granting us the faith to believe in our risen Lord, enabling us to experience his presence.**

Collect

Eternal God our heavenly Father, who reveals your risen Son to those who are willing to see with the eyes of faith: Touch our hearts with a vision of Christ; that we may have the joy of a firsthand experience with our risen Lord, through whom we pray. Amen.

Prayer of Confession

We picture in our minds, Father, the excitement of the disciples when they saw the risen Lord. But that leaves us with a secondhand experience, because we do not include ourselves in that scene. Forgive us when we fail to see, in our day-by-day experiences, the risen Lord going with us. Increase our faith, that we, too, may know the Lord is risen because of his presence with us. In his name we pray. Amen.

Hymns

"I Know That My Redeemer Lives"
"O Holy Savior, Friend Unseen"
"Strong Son of God, Immortal Love"
"Thine Is the Glory"

THIRD SUNDAY OF EASTER

First Lesson: Acts 3:12-19
Theme: God will forgive our rejection of Jesus

Call to Worship

Pastor: We worship our Lord Jesus Christ, who was crucified, dead, and buried, but who arose from the dead.

People: **Jesus died because sinners like ourselves rejected him.**

Pastor: God knows what we have done, and desires to forgive us if we will repent of our sins.

People: **Praise God for our living Savior, and for his forgiving love!**

Collect

Gracious Father, who forgives us for rejecting your Son if we return in true repentance: Reveal to us the many ways in which we continue to crucify our Lord, that we may repent of our sin and receive your forgiveness. In our Savior's name we pray. Amen.

Prayer of Confession

We grieve at the way Jesus was treated, Father, and wish people had been more responsive to his mission. Yet we, too, are guilty of rejecting Jesus, not with a cross, but with our indifference and self-righteousness. Forgive us when we shut Jesus out of our lives, even as we claim to be your children. Help us to commit ourselves in complete surrender to Christ, that we may serve him with our lives rather than reject him. In his name we pray. Amen.

Hymns

"Depth of Mercy"
"Jesus, Thy Blood and Righteousness"
"Sinners, Turn: Why Will You Die"
"Where Shall My Wondering Soul Begin"

THIRD SUNDAY OF EASTER

Second Lesson: 1 John 3:1-7
Theme: We are God's children

Call to Worship

Leader: We are the children of God. Therefore let us worship him with sincere hearts.

People: We are God's children because he loves us; and we worship God, because we love him as our Father.

Leader: As children of God, we are challenged to live like Jesus in witness of God's fatherhood.

People: May we worship God each day as we live in obedience to our heavenly Father.

Collect

Heavenly Father, who created us in your image, and then reclaimed us as your children by the mercy of your great love expressed in your Son, Jesus: Give us the desire to be like Jesus, that we may offer to you the purity of those who desire to be called your children. Hear us for Jesus' sake. Amen.

Prayer of Confession

Dear God, we call on you as our Father, expecting you to hear us and help us. That implies we consider ourselves to be your children, but our lives do not speak well of being your offspring. Forgive us when our independence convinces us we can live as we please and still claim all the privileges of being your children. Inspire us to follow the example of Jesus' life, that we may give honor and glory to you. We pray through Christ our Lord. Amen.

Hymns

"Come, Ye (We) That Love the Lord"
"I Want A Principle Within"
"I Would Be True"
"Take Time to Be Holy"

THIRD SUNDAY OF EASTER

Gospel: Luke 24:35-48
Theme: Jesus appears to his disciples

Call to Worship

Pastor: The risen Christ appeared to his disciples with the assurance that the Scriptures had been fulfilled.
People: The purpose of his life, death, and resurrection was to share God's message of forgiveness.
Pastor: The risen Christ still commissions his followers to be his witnesses, calling all people to repentance.
People: We serve the risen Christ, and take up the call to repentance, that all may hear of God's forgiveness.

Collect

Almighty God, whose risen Son calls his followers to go forth as his witnesses: Use your church today to lead our world to repentance, that all may experience your forgiveness. We pray through Christ, our risen Lord. Amen.

Prayer of Confession

We never cease to be amazed, Father, with the resurrection of your Son. But we are more amazed at life after death than the purpose of his resurrection. Forgive us when our devotion to the glory of his resurrection hinders us in witnessing to your message of salvation. Use us to share the good news of your forgiveness, that we may encourage many to repent from their sins. In our Savior's name we pray. Amen.

Hymns

"O Master of the Waking World"
"We Believe in One True God"
"We've a Story to Tell to the Nations"
"Ye Servants of God"

FOURTH SUNDAY OF EASTER

First Lesson: Acts 4:8-12
Theme: Jesus is our only Savior

Call to Worship

Pastor: Let us join in a celebration of Christ our Savior who makes us whole!

People: Praise be to Jesus, who died on the cross, and arose from the grave to give us victory over sin!

Pastor: Jesus alone is our Savior, for no one else is able to give us atonement with God.

People: We commit our love and devotion to Jesus, who alone cleanses us from sin and gives us a new life.

Collect

Heavenly Father, who has given your Son, Jesus, as our only Savior to bring us into your presence as people made whole: Refine our faith of any impure confidences, that we may put our whole trust only in Jesus, and be delivered from our sin. In his name we pray. Amen.

Prayer of Confession

Jesus is Lord! We believe that, Father, but we live in an age that questions the unique position of Jesus. In our acceptance of people of other religions, we find ourselves questioning that basic article of our faith. Forgive us when we lose sight of what you have done for all persons through Jesus alone. Reestablish us in our faith; that we may know salvation is ours only because of your gift of Jesus, in whose name we pray. Amen.

Hymns

"All Hail the Power of Jesus' Name"
"All Praise to Thee, for Thou, O King Divine"
"At the Name of Jesus"
"Take the Name of Jesus with You"

FOURTH SUNDAY OF EASTER

Second Lesson: 1 John 3:18-24
Theme: Life which demonstrates God's indwelling Spirit

Call to Worship
Pastor: The Christian faith is more than just feelings we have in our hearts.
People: The Christian faith is a way of life in which we live by the convictions we feel.
Pastor: Such life brings us in union with God in which he blesses us with his presence.
People: May the words we express in worship bear the fruit of a life lived in obedience to God.

Collect
O loving God our heavenly Father, who dwells in the hearts of those who live in obedience to your commands: Cause our faith to become our way of life; that we may enjoy the blessing of living in union with you through your Son Jesus Christ, in whose name we pray. Amen.

Prayer of Confession
Our lips are familiar with the words of religious ritual, Father, and we are able to make our faith sound devout. But the life we live is not always in harmony with the faith we profess. Forgive us when our faith is without works, and our belief is not demonstrated by obedience. Help us to live a life which is true to our faith, that we may experience a fellowship of love with one another, and with you. We pray through Christ our Lord. Amen.

Hymns
"O Come, and Dwell in Me"
"Spirit of Faith, Come Down"
"Truehearted, Wholehearted"
"When We Walk with the Lord"

FOURTH SUNDAY OF EASTER

Gospel: John 10:11-18
Theme: The Good Shepherd

Call to Worship

Leader: We worship Jesus who, like a good shepherd, laid down his life for us.
People: We worship Jesus who, like a good shepherd, knows each of us personally.
Leader: We worship Jesus who, like a good shepherd, loves others whom he would like to bring into his fold.
People: We worship Jesus, our Good Shepherd, and give ourselves in obedience to his will.

Collect

Compassionate Father, whose Son gave himself in a ministry of loving care and redeeming grace: Bring us into his fold; that we may feel the blessing of his life restoring us to wholeness and protecting us from being ravaged by sin. We pray in our Savior's name. Amen.

Prayer of Confession

We wander around in life, Father, and try to convince ourselves it is a wonderful adventure. But we are lost, and cannot find our way. Forgive us when we lay aside self-discipline, divine guidance, and common sense in an attempt to find ourselves. Draw us closer to Christ, that we may understand his guiding presence in our lives which will keep us in his care. In his name we pray. Amen.

Hymns

"All the Way, My Savior Leads Me"
"He Leadeth Me: O Blessed Thought"
"Savior, Like a Shepherd Lead Us"
"Shepherd of Eager Youth"

FIFTH SUNDAY OF EASTER

First Lesson: Acts 8:26-40
Theme: Strength through fellowship with believers

Call to Worship

Leader: Greetings in the name of Christ to all who are called by his name!

People: May the peace of Christ be in our hearts as we share our faith with one another.

Leader: We are one in Christ, united to give and receive mutual strength to each other's faith.

People: May the Holy Spirit keep us true in our devotion to Christ as we encourage one another in the Christian life.

Collect

Heavenly Father, who strengthens us in our faith through the fellowship of Christian friends: Bind us together in true love and appreciation for one another, that we may each contribute to a growing faith in all who join our fellowship. We pray through Christ our Lord. Amen.

Prayer of Confession

Forgive us, Father, when our faith has grown cold by our indifference to the fellowship of Christian friends. Our schedules are full, and we seem to cut out church activities first. Then, before we know it, we lose the zeal of a vital faith, and life itself loses its vitality. Give us a warm personality which makes us seek out the companionship of those who believe in Christ, that we may give as well as receive the human support which the community of believers needs. We pray in Jesus' name. Amen.

Hymns

"All Praise to Our Redeeming Lord"
"Blest Be the Dear Uniting Love"
"Blest Be the Tie that Binds"
"Jesus, United by Thy Grace"

FIFTH SUNDAY OF EASTER

Second Lesson: 1 John 4:7-12
Theme: God is love, so love one another

Call to Worship
Pastor: If we are God's children, we will love one another, because God is love.
People: Love for one another is evidence that we know the love God gives to us.
Pastor: Divine love restores life. God's love gives us new life through his Son, Jesus.
People: Praise God for his love which gives us new life in Christ! May we follow his example in loving one another.

Collect
O loving Father, who loves us enough to give us redemption through your only Son, Jesus: Grant us new life in Christ, that we may give evidence to your great love by loving one another as you have loved us. We pray in our Savior's name. Amen.

Prayer of Confession
We talk about love quite freely, Father, and praise you for your love. But it is much easier to talk about love than it is to love those with whom we talk. Forgive us when we sound so loving in our discussions, and then live as if we do not know how to love. Help us to receive in our hearts the love you give through Jesus, that our lives may tell the story of your love. We pray through Christ our Lord. Amen.

Hymns
"Blest Be the Dear Uniting Love"
"Blest Be the Tie that Binds"
"God Is Love; His Mercy Brightens"
"What Wondrous Love Is This"

FIFTH SUNDAY OF EASTER

Gospel: John 15:1-8
Theme: Jesus is the true vine

Call to Worship

Pastor: We come together from many different places; but we are a part of each other, because we all belong to Christ.
People: We are like many branches of one vine; and Christ is that vine, uniting us to himself.
Pastor: We are united to Christ so that he may work through us to bear fruit in his kingdom.
People: We pray that many persons will be brought into God's kingdom because of our relationship with Christ.

Collect

Almighty God, whose Son desires that we remain in union with him for the purpose of bearing fruit in your kingdom: Keep us faithful to our Lord and Savior, that our witness may influence others to accept Christ as their Savior. In his name we pray. Amen.

Prayer of Confession

Dear Father, we are followers of your Son, Jesus; but much of our following is often from a distance. And so our discipleship does not bear much fruit. Forgive us when we have been satisfied with appearing to be Christian, without bearing the fruit of Christian discipleship. Unite us to Christ in a strong bond of love and loyalty, that the fruit of our labors may bring glory to you. We pray through Christ our Lord. Amen.

Hymns

"Blest Be the Dear Uniting Love"
"Draw Thou My Soul, O Christ"
"Have Thine Own Way, Lord"
"I Need Thee Every Hour"

SIXTH SUNDAY OF EASTER

First Lesson: Acts 11:19-30
Theme: The Gentile mission

Call to Worship
Pastor: The church is the body of Christ, made up of all persons who serve Jesus as Lord and Savior.
People: All national and geographical differences are overcome by God's gift of his Spirit.
Pastor: The Holy Spirit refreshes the lives of all who will repent, and put their trust in Jesus Christ.
People: We praise God for giving his love to all persons through his Son, Jesus, Savior of the world!

Collect
Heavenly Father, who has included all persons in your invitation to new life through your Son, Jesus: Increase our love which we express through Christian fellowship and witness, that your church may effectively share the Gospel with all persons. In our Savior's name we pray. Amen.

Prayer of Confession
We profess to be mission minded, Father, and pray for the church world wide. But much of the love we share is confined to an offering envelope to help people we do not really care to know. Forgive us for prejudices which keep us from being a loving church which is truly united in Christ throughout the world. Give us your Spirit; and enable us to understand that same Spirit is given to all who are your children. Thus may we heal the fractures and divisions in your church, the living body of Christ, through whom we pray. Amen.

Hymns
"All Praise to Our Redeeming Lord"
"Blest Be the Tie that Binds"
"Christ for the World We Sing"
"We've A Story to Tell to the Nations"

SIXTH SUNDAY OF EASTER

Second Lesson: 1 John 5:1-6
Theme: Victory over the world

Call to Worship
Pastor: Jesus is the Son of God. Believe that, and you are a child of God!
People: We do believe Jesus is God's Son. And we believe he is our Lord and Savior.
Pastor: Faith like that gives us victory over sin and death. Our Lord's triumph becomes ours!
People: We rejoice in our victory which Christ, our risen Lord, shares with us!

Collect
Almighty God, who enables us to overcome the evil of this world by faith in your Son, Jesus: Feed our faith daily by the inspiration of our risen Lord, that we may win a victory over all sin with which our world may tempt us. We pray through Christ our Lord. Amen.

Prayer of Confession
We continue to rejoice in Christ's victory over death, our Father. But we do not feel as victorious as those who believe in him ought to feel. Forgive us when we fail to grow in faith, not trusting in the power you provide through Christ to defeat the threat of sin. Give us the joy of victory by renewed faith in your Son, Jesus, who rose from the grave to give us a triumphant life. In his name we pray. Amen.

Hymns
"Be Thou My Vision"
"Fight the Good Fight"
"I Know Not Why God's Wondrous Grace"
"Soldiers of Christ, Arise"

SIXTH SUNDAY OF EASTER

Gospel: John 15:9-17
Theme: The ministry of love

Call to Worship

Leader: We worship our Savior, Jesus Christ, who loves us even as God loved him.
People: Jesus was obedient to his Father, and remained in his love.
Leader: Jesus challenges us to remain in his love by obeying his teachings.
People: Jesus has taught us to love one another as he has loved us. May God help us bear that kind of fruit in our lives.

Collect

Gracious Father, whose Son loved you enough to love us in our sin: Give us hearts capable of loving and being loved; that we may be obedient to the command of our Savior, Jesus Christ, in whose name we pray. Amen.

Prayer of Confession

We come in confession of our disobedience to our Lord's command to love one another, Father. We choose friends; but these are few, because we are not able to love as we are loved by our Savior. Forgive us for hindering the growth of your church and the joy of our friendship by restricting our love. Recreate us to be self-giving persons who are able to love; that we may become true friends of Christ, and true friends of all your children. In our Savior's name we pray. Amen.

Hymns

"At Length There Dawns the Glorious Day"
"Eternal Son, Eternal Love"
"Jesus, United by Thy Grace"
"O Brother Man, Fold to Thy Heart"

ASCENSION DAY
(Or the Sunday Nearest)

First Lesson: Acts 1:1-11
Theme: The ascension of Jesus

Call to Worship
Pastor: Lift up your hearts in praise for our Savior whom God lifted into heaven!
People: We praise Jesus, our exalted Savior who is at the right hand of God the Father!
Pastor: Jesus has not left us, because he lives in our hearts; and we are witnesses of the new life he brings.
People: Glory be to Christ, God's Word made flesh, who manifests God's love to us!

Collect
Almighty God, whose Son ascended into heaven after his earthly life, instructing his disciples to be his witnesses: Inspire us with your Holy Spirit, that we may be filled with power to witness to the new life our Lord gives. In his name we pray. Amen.

Prayer of Confession
Father, we know you have exalted Christ in the highest heaven, with glory beyond anything we can comprehend. But we confess we have not exalted Christ within our own hearts. Forgive us when we take control of our lives instead of letting Christ be our authority. Give us the surrender which will let Christ lead us in a new life, enabling us to be faithful witnesses to the saved life which our Lord makes available to all persons. In his name we pray. Amen.

Hymns
"All Hail the Power of Jesus' Name"
"Crown Him with Many Crowns"
"Look, Ye Saints! The Sight Is Glorious"
"O For a Thousand Tongues to Sing"

ASCENSION DAY
(Or the Sunday Nearest)

Second Lesson: Ephesians 1:15-23
Theme: The exalted Christ

Call to Worship

Pastor: Christ our Lord has been exalted by God his Father, and rules with supreme authority.

People: We give Christ the highest praise, for worthy indeed is he who brought salvation!

Pastor: Christ has all authority over the church which continues to fulfill his mission of salvation.

People: How very great is the wonderful work Christ performs through his church!

Collect

Eternal God, whose exalted Son is the supreme ruler of our lives, and head of the church: Accept our humble devotion to serve him as his church, that your power may transform our commitment into a mighty force bringing your salvation to our world. In our Savior's name we pray. Amen.

Prayer of Confession

With great power, O God, you have given us your Son as our Savior. You raised him from death, and have exalted him with the highest honor. With that same power, you minister to our world through the church, the body of Christ. Forgive us, Father, when we become so indifferent to what it means to be the church, ministering in the name of our Savior. Strengthen us by your Spirit, to become the church which demonstrates a living Lord with power to redeem. In his name we pray. Amen.

Hymns

"All Praise to Thee, for Thou, O King Divine"
"Majestic Sweetness Sits Enthroned"
"The Church's One Foundation"
"The Head That Once Was Crowned"

ASCENSION DAY
(Or the Sunday Nearest)

Gospel: Mark 16:9-16, 19-20 (or Luke 24:46-53)
Theme: The great commission

Call to Worship

Pastor: We are sent people, because our Lord's last words were a charge to preach the gospel to all mankind.
People: We have a message of salvation for all who will believe and be baptized.
Pastor: The body of believers is a powerful witness to God's redeeming love in Christ.
People: May all we do as Christ's church be done in Jesus' name, giving honor and glory to him.

Collect

Father in heaven, whose Son continues to reach mankind today through his body of believers: Make us effective witnesses on his behalf, that many may believe and be baptized into salvation. In our Savior's name we pray. Amen.

Prayer of Confession

We believe in spreading your good news, Father, so that all may hear, and be saved. But we support a few in their witnessing, rather than be witnesses ourselves. Forgive us when you have depended on our personal witness to win someone else, and we have failed. Give us the desire to let our lives be a means of interpreting the gospel to others; that we may not prevent anyone from believing in Christ, through whom we pray. Amen.

Hymns

"Christ for the World We Sing"
"Go Make of All Disciples"
"O Zion, Haste"
"We've A Story to Tell to the Nations"

SEVENTH SUNDAY OF EASTER

First Lesson: Acts 1:15-17, 21-26
Theme: Matthias replaces Judas

Call to Worship
Pastor: Hear the invitation: Come and be a disciple of the risen Lord!
People: We are unworthy because of sin. But we are eligible, because we know our Lord's redemption.
Pastor: We become effective disciples when we live in commitment to Christ and in fellowship with those who serve him.
People: We feel called to serve our Lord, and pray that we may be faithful to our calling.

Collect
Eternal God, who is constantly calling persons into Christian discipleship as witnesses of our risen Lord: Inspire us to be faithful in our devotion to Christ; that our discipleship may give a faithful witness of salvation in Jesus, our Savior, through whom we pray. Amen.

Prayer of Confession
We consider ourselves to be Christian disciples, Father; but we feel it is more by our choice, than our being called into service. So when we do not choose as strongly to serve Christ, we do not feel we have neglected a special call. Forgive us when we are undependable in our discipleship and sporadic in our service. Convict us of apathy, and convince us of faithfulness; that we may be firmly established as disciples of Christ, in whose name we pray. Amen.

Hymns
"A Charge to Keep I Have"
"Jesus Calls Us O'er the Tumult"
"O Jesus, I Have Promised"
"O Master, Let Me Walk with Thee"

SEVENTH SUNDAY OF EASTER

Second Lesson: 1 John 5:9-13
Theme: Jesus is our source of life

Call to Worship
Pastor: We have gathered for worship. Let us proclaim our faith in Christ.
People: We believe Jesus is the Son of God, who died that we might be forgiven to live a new life with God!
Pastor: Such faith brings us in union with God our Father to experience life at its best.
People: Our life is in Christ. May we so live that others, too, may believe in the Son of God.

Collect
Wonderful God, our Father, who dwells in the hearts of those who believe in Jesus, your Son, blessing us with new life: Keep us ever faithful to your son; that we may enjoy your gift of life, not only now, but in eternity. In our Savior's name we pray. Amen.

Prayer of Confession
We are your church, O God, living examples of your Son, our Savior. But sometimes we are satisfied with only our knowledge of Christ instead of our experience. Forgive us for knowledge we have received that we have not put into practice in our lives. Help us to receive your Son both into our minds and in our hearts; that we may have the life only he can give. In his name we pray. Amen.

Hymns
"Father, I Stretch My Hands to Thee"
"Jesus Is All the World to Me"
"Take My Life, and Let It Be Consecrated"
"Thou Art the Way: To Thee Alone"

SEVENTH SUNDAY OF EASTER

Gospel: John 17:11b-19
Theme: Jesus' prayer for his disciples

Call to Worship

Leader: Jesus consecrated himself to his redemptive act on the cross, that we might consecrate our lives to God.

People: **We feel God helping us live the Christian life in a world of temptation.**

Leader: When Jesus consecrated himself, he asked God to undergird his followers with strength and loyalty.

People: **We thank God for his help, and dedicate ourselves to faithfulness.**

Collect

Almighty God, who keeps your children safe from the power of evil through the sacrifice of your only Son: Keep us loyal to our Savior, Jesus Christ; that we may be consecrated to a life of purity and righteousness, filled with the joy of those who belong to you. We pray in Jesus' name. Amen.

Prayer of Confession

We are willing Christians, Father, when it comes to taking the name of Christ. But we find many excuses when it comes to living a consecrated life. Forgive us when we avoid the dedication for which Christ prayed and died. Protect us from the temptation of insincere faith and uncommitted living. Take hold of our beings, and make us wholly yours, that we may be dedicated living witnesses of our Savior Jesus Christ, in whose name we pray. Amen.

Hymns

"Draw Thou My Soul, O Christ"
"Make Me a Captive, Lord"
"More Love to Thee, O Christ"
"Take My Life, and Let It Be Consecrated"

THE DAY OF PENTECOST

First Lesson: Ezekiel 37:1-14
Theme: The hope of restored life

Call to Worship
Pastor: Today is a celebration of new life.
People: We celebrate the life God's Spirit has breathed into the church throughout its history.
Pastor: God's Spirit has also breathed new life into our souls throughout our personal history.
People: We celebrate life, thanking God for the breath of his Spirit that makes living worthwhile.

Collect
Gracious Father, who restores life to your people through the breath of your Spirit: Breathe upon your church today; that we may come alive with all our energies to serve as living disciples of your Son, our Savior, through whom we pray. Amen.

Prayer of Confession
Father, we often become discouraged with the lack of influence the church has in our world. We wonder if our task is greater than our abilities. But then we remember the promise and power of your Spirit and realize we are not alone in our mission. Forgive us for our neglect of your Spirit when we work so hard without your guidance. Revive your church with new life to be the body of Christ in today's world. In his name we pray. Amen.

Hymns
"Christ Is Made the Sure Foundation"
"God of Grace and God of Glory"
"O God, Our Help in Ages Past"
"Spirit of Life in This New Dawn"

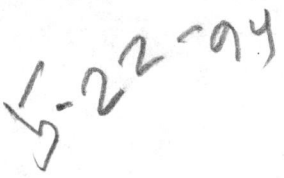

THE DAY OF PENTECOST

Second Lesson: Acts 2:1-21 (or Romans 8:22-27)
Theme: The descent of the Holy Spirit at Pentecost

Call to Worship

Pastor: The church is a spiritual fellowship through which the risen Christ communicates his saving grace.

People: We are born of the Spirit, not by our own doing, but by the power and love of God.

Pastor: His Spirit is the source of our being, and the means by which we are able to share the gospel of Jesus Christ.

People: We pray that we may be receptive to the guidance of the Holy Spirit, that our witness may communicate the Savior's love to our world.

Collect

Almighty God, who has inspired your church in each generation through the gift of your Holy Spirit: Grant us the power to share the good news of Christ effectively; that those who hear may know what you have done through Jesus our Lord, in whose name we pray. Amen.

Prayer of Confession

We are your church, O God, but we fear we have made it more an organization than a spiritual force to bring our world into reconciliation with you. Forgive us when we open our lives to your love and close our hearts to the ministry for which your Holy Spirit would equip us. Break through the barriers our human nature creates in your church, and fill us with power and love to share the salvation our Lord has provided. In his name we pray. Amen.

Hymns

"Come, Holy Spirit, Heavenly Dove"
"Holy Ghost, Dispel Our Sadness"
"Spirit Divine, Attend Our Prayers"
"Spirit of God, Descend upon My Heart"

THE DAY OF PENTECOST

Gospel: John 15:26-27; 16:4b-15
Theme: Jesus promises the Spirit of Truth

Call to Worship

Leader: Jesus promised that God would reveal his truth through the Holy Spirit.
People: We do not know everything about God, but we do know the Holy Spirit inspires us with a truth which convicts us of sin.
Leader: The law is limited in what it can reveal as right and wrong. But we all know the Holy Spirit convicts us of truth which the law cannot express.
People: We trust God to lead us by his Spirit in a life which reveals the way of truth.

Collect

Heavenly Father, whose nature and will is perfect truth; and who imparts that truth to us through the Holy Spirit: Inspire us with pure intentions and desires, that we may give an honest witness to the life which you desire all people to live. In our Savior's name we pray. Amen.

Prayer of Confession

We are people who are prone to sin, Father, but we defend ourselves by trying to make our sins look right, rather than confessing we are wrong. Forgive us for avoiding the conviction of our sins which you reveal through the Holy Spirit. Guide us in the true way to live; that we may benefit by the redeeming love of Christ our Savior, in whose name we pray. Amen.

Hymns

"Breathe on Me, Breath of God"
"God of All Power and Truth and Grace"
"Holy Spirit, Truth Divine"
"Spirit of Faith, Come Down"

FIRST SUNDAY AFTER PENTECOST
(Trinity Sunday)

First Lesson: Isaiah 6:1-8
Theme: God's call to service

Call to Worship

Pastor [Leader]: Holy, holy, holy is the Lord, God almighty!
People: The whole earth is full of his glory.
Pastor [Leader]: Yet we have dared to come into his presence with praise and confession, to be commissioned in his service.
People: Here we are for God to use us as he sees fit.

Collect

Holy God, our Father, who has called us into your presence to share our adoration and devotion: Grant us your Spirit, undergirding us, in whatever you call us to do; that we may not fail in our service of Christ, your Son, in whose name we pray. Amen.

Prayer of Confession

How often we have been here, Father, and have taken your presence for granted. Yet we did not hear your call to service, nor did we expect it. Forgive us when we have concluded our worship services instead of going out to begin our services. Keep us mindful of your holy presence in all we do; that life itself may be our worship of you. In our Savior's name we pray. Amen.

Hymns

"Forth in Thy Name"
"God of Grace and God of Glory"
"Holy, Holy, Holy"
"I Love to Tell the Story"

FIRST SUNDAY AFTER PENTECOST
(Trinity Sunday)

Second Lesson: Romans 8:12-17
Theme: Led by God's Spirit

Call to Worship

Pastor: We become God's children when we let his Spirit lead us.

People: Our sinful nature is strong, but God is our Father and defends us against sin by his Spirit.

Pastor: As God's Children we are assured that we shall possess eternal life which God gives through his Son, Jesus.

People: We trust God to lead us in a life of victory over sin and death.

Collect

Eternal God, who enables us by your Spirit to become your children: Inspire us to put to death our sinful desires; that we may call you our Father, and receive the blessing kept for those who are your children. We pray through Christ our Lord. Amen.

Prayer of Confession

Gracious Father, we are your children because you have created us. But we deny your fatherhood by our sinful behavior. We feel your Spirit directing us, and we turn the other way. We call you our Father, not because we live as your children, but because we want what you have to offer. Forgive us for our waywardness which brings us to you for selfish reasons only. Fill us with your Spirit, that our lives may proclaim you as our Father because of our love and loyalty. In our Savior's name we pray. Amen.

Hymns

"Be Thou My Vision"
"Come, Holy Spirit, Heavenly Dove"
"Lead Us, O Father"
"Spirit of God, Descend upon My Heart"

FIRST SUNDAY AFTER PENTECOST
(Trinity Sunday)

Gospel: John 3:1-17
Theme: Born of the Spirit

Call to Worship
Pastor: Because of parents, we have life. Because of God, we have new life.
People: We are born again when God breathes his Spirit upon us, as though it were the beginning of a new life.
Pastor: Our conversion to the Christian faith is like that. We live a new life, led by God's Spirit.
People: May the Spirit of God breathe new life into our souls, that we may enter God's kingdom.

Collect
O God, our loving Father, who breathes new life into our souls by the gift of your Holy Spirit: Grant us your Spirit; that we may be born anew to live in the joy of salvation through Christ our Redeemer, in whose name we pray. Amen.

Prayer of Confession
We live from one day to the next, Father; but many times we feel we are existing rather than living. Our natural inclination to sin imprisons us in our physical world, preventing us from being born of the Spirit. Forgive us for narrowing life to the world of flesh and its desires. Open our hearts to the gift of your Spirit, that we may come alive with the joy of salvation. In our Savior's name we pray. Amen.

Hymns
"Breathe On Me, Breath of God"
"Father, I Stretch My Hands to Thee"
"Holy Ghost, Dispel Our Sadness"
"Holy Spirit, Truth Divine"

PROPER 4
Sunday between May 29 and June 4 inclusive
(If after Trinity Sunday)

First Lesson: 1 Samuel 16:1-13
Theme: David selected to succeed Saul

Call to Worship
Pastor: It is a wonderful thing to be chosen by God for his service.
People: When God calls, it is a privilege to give ourselves on his behalf.
Pastor: God chooses us, not because of our importance, but because of his need.
People: May we always see our service in the church as a calling of God; and be ready to serve as he demands.

Collect
Heavenly Father, who calls us into your service: Keep us mindful of who we are, what we are to do, and why we are to do it; that we may live a life of service on your behalf. In our Savior's name we pray. Amen.

Prayer of Confession
We are busy people, Father, and have good reasons for not doing more in the church than what we are doing. When we do work, our motivation is usually less than a divine call. Forgive us when we have not acted as servants on your behalf; and have seen our work as an unrewarding end in itself. Choose us as you see fit, and inspire us to do our best for your honor and glory. In Jesus' name we pray. Amen.

Hymns
"Forth in Thy Name"
"Lord, Speak to Me"
"O Jesus, I Have Promised"
"The Voice of God Is Calling"

PROPER 4
Sunday between May 29 and June 4 inclusive
(If after Trinity Sunday)

Second Lesson: 2 Corinthians 4:5-12
Theme: Our weakness demonstrates God's power

Call to Worship
Pastor: The church is people who are mortal, and therefore weak compared to the mighty power of God.
People: **Our weakness is often revealed when we struggle with the problems of our world.**
Pastor: But our weakness also demonstrates that it is God's power which makes us, who are weak, victorious!
People: **We commit ourselves to be instruments of God, that our weakness may reveal true victory in Jesus Christ.**

Collect
Almighty God, who uses the weakness of our mortal nature to demonstrate your redemptive power: Convince us that, defeated as we sometimes feel, our weakness reveals your greatness; so that in spite of personal limitations and failures, you may gain a great victory over the power of sin. In our Savior's name we pray. Amen.

Prayer of Confession
We aim for greatness in the church, Father, even though we must confess we are weak against the force of evil. And that goal deceives our faith. Forgive us when we interpret apparent defeat as a poor witness to your mighty presence in our world. Help us to give ourselves to you, in trouble or adversity, confident that such situations will reveal your power and love. We pray through Christ our Lord. Amen.

Hymns
"Am I a Soldier of the Cross"
"Fight the Good Fight"
"God Is My Strong Salvation"
"He Who Would Valiant Be"

PROPER 4
Sunday between May 29 and June 4 inclusive
(If after Trinity Sunday)

Gospel: Mark 2:23 — 3:6
Theme: The Sabbath, a symbol of salvation

Call to Worship

Pastor: This is the Lord's Day, a day to worship God in thanksgiving for our salvation.
People: We praise God for the victory over sin which he gives through his Son, Jesus Christ!
Pastor: We are freed from the bondage of sin; and this day is a public witness of how God has saved us.
People: May this day be a weekly symbol to our world that God has made us free. We rejoice in him!

Collect

Most holy Father, who has come in our midst to save us, and has set this day aside as a symbol of salvation to our society: Grant that we may live this one day in such a way as to give you honor and glory for our salvation in Jesus Christ, through whom we pray. Amen.

Prayer of Confession

We recall, Father, how we used to dread Sunday because of all the restrictions. Yet in our present freedom from those restrictions we feel we have also lost the purpose for calling this your day. Forgive us when we fail to let this first day of the week be a symbol of the salvation you have given through your Son. Direct us in our activities, that we may not misrepresent the salvation of which this day speaks. We pray through Christ our Lord. Amen.

Hymns

"Come, Let Us Tune Our Loftiest Song"
"Jesus, We Want to Meet"
"O Day of Rest and Gladness"
"Safely Through Another Week"

PROPER 5
Sunday between June 5 and 11 inclusive
(If after Trinity Sunday)

First Lesson: 1 Samuel 16:14-23
Theme: The peace of God

Call to Worship
Pastor: Life can be quite a battle field with all its struggles and conflicts!
People: There are many times when we need to be able to get in touch with God, and find his peace to calm our souls.
Pastor: God's peace is always available to us for whatever circumstances life may bring.
People: May God's Spirit rest upon us with the blessing of his peace throughout our days.

Collect
Heavenly Father, who desires to bring peace to our troubled souls: Come to us through your Spirit, and bring calm to our distress; that we may enjoy the life you want us to live. In the name of Christ we pray. Amen.

Prayer of Confession
We are too familiar with distress, Father, from all the responsibility and frustration we have. But we know we do not need to be overcome with our distress. Forgive us when we make life a struggle, instead of living victoriously in the blessing of your peace. Give us that victory now, as we yield ourselves to you. We pray in Jesus' name. Amen.

Hymns
"Be Not Dismayed"
"Come, Ye Disconsolate"
"Peace, Perfect Peace"
"When the Storms of Life are Raging"

PROPER 5
Sunday between June 5 and 11 inclusive
(If after Trinity Sunday)

Second Lesson: 2 Corinthians 4:13 — 5:1
Theme: Live by faith

Call to Worship
Pastor: Life brings us trouble and pain. But our faith convinces us of our eternal glory which is much greater than the trials of this temporary life.
People: **We live by faith, believing God blesses us with much more than what this world can give.**
Pastor: Our physical life will end, but we know God will bless us with life that goes on forever!
People: **We do not fear the suffering of this life, because we look forward to eternal joy where there will be no pain or sorrow!**

Collect
Gracious Father, who has prepared for us the eternal blessings of love, joy, and peace: Encourage us in the difficulties of this life, that we may not lose sight of these unseen blessings which last forever. We pray through Christ our Lord. Amen.

Prayer of Confession
Life hurts us many times, Father, and we feel defeated. We look only at our present situation, and sometimes it overwhelms us. Forgive us when our faith is so weak that we fail to see the real life which you are offering to us. Give us a vision of the unseen reality of an eternal joy where we are forever at home in the security of your love. In our Savior's name we pray. Amen.

Hymns
"Be Thou My Vision"
"O Gracious Father of Mankind"
"O Holy Savior, Friend Unseen"
"Open My Eyes, That I May See"

PROPER 5
Sunday between June 5 and 11 inclusive
(If after Trinity Sunday)

Gospel: Mark 3:20-35
Theme: Sin against the Holy Spirit

Call to Worship

Pastor: Holy is the Lord, Father Almighty, who made heaven and earth.

People: We give praise to God, our Creator, Redeemer, and Judge.

Pastor: The holiness of God is the source of our salvation from sin. To deny God's holiness is to be judged guilty of sin.

People: Our faith is in Christ Jesus who has demonstrated the power, love and authority of the holy God, our heavenly Father.

Collect

Heavenly Father, whose holiness is not to be challenged or denied: Convince us by your Holy Spirit of our sinfulness and your redemptive love, that we may not be judged guilty of denying your righteous authority over our lives. We pray through Christ our Redeemer. Amen.

Prayer of Confession

We believe your grace is great enough to remove the guilt of our sins, Father. Yet, in our careless way of living, we take lightly your holiness, and the authority you have to judge us. Forgive us if we have acted willfully or unwillfully in any way which suggests we do not acknowledge your holiness or authority. Cleanse us by the blood of Christ our Savior, and lead us in a life which gives glory and praise to you. In our Savior's name we pray. Amen.

Hymns

"Holy God, We Praise Thy Name"
"Holy, Holy, Holy! Lord God Almighty"
"Love Divine, All Loves Excelling"
"Take Time to Be Holy"

PROPER 6
Sunday between June 12 and 18 inclusive
(If after Trinity Sunday)

First Lesson: 2 Samuel 1:1, 17-27
Theme: David's lament over Saul and Jonathan

Call to Worship
Pastor: Grief is a part of our humanness we must live with.
People: It is a painful experience when we lose a loved one in death.
Pastor: Our grief is softened when we take it to the Lord, who gives the comfort of his Spirit.
People: We are thankful for the healing God gives to us in our grief when we share it with him.

Collect
Gracious Father, who knows the pain we suffer when a loved one dies: Send your Spirit to all who mourn; that they may find comfort for their sorrow; and be strengthed in their faith. We pray in the name of Christ our Lord. Amen.

Prayer of Confession
Father, we confess our weakness in accepting the death of our loved ones. Thank you for the hope you have given us through your risen Son. Forgive us when we are so grieved that we resist the comfort of your Spirit. When in sorrow, lift us by your Spirit to know you are sharing our pain with us. In our Savior's name, we pray. Amen.

Hymns
"Abide with Me"
"I Know Not What the Future Hath"
"On Jordan's Stormy Banks I Stand"
"Sing with All the Sons of Glory"

PROPER 6
Sunday between June 12 and 18 inclusive
(If after Trinity Sunday)

Second Lesson: 2 Corinthians 5:6-10, 14-17
Theme: Encouraged by our faith

Call to Worship
Pastor: The Christian life is not a means of material gain, but a source of spiritual blessing.
People: We enjoy the physical life God gives, but our faith assures an even fuller life for those who are faithful to God.
Pastor: Faith gives us courage when fear would discourage us, for we know Christ is our source of strength.
People: Praise God for faith through which he grants us courage to be Christians!

Collect
Gracious Father, who encourages us to live by faith in your Son, our Savior: Increase our faith to be loyal disciples, that we may be strengthened against adversity and give a true witness to your love and power. We pray through Christ our Lord. Amen.

Prayer of Confession
We know the pain of discouragement, Father, because we put so much confidence in the happiness of this world. Forgive us when we lose sight of the spiritual world and lose courage to resist the influence of this world. Bless us with your presence as a means of strengthening our faith; that we may learn to live courageously, and please you with our discipleship. Hear us for Jesus' sake. Amen.

Hymns
"God of Grace and God of Glory"
"He Who Would Valiant Be"
"March On, O Soul, with Strength"
"O For a Faith that Will Not Shrink"

PROPER 6
Sunday between June 12 and 18 inclusive
(If after Trinity Sunday)
Gospel: Mark 4:26-34
Theme: Parables of the Kingdom

Call to Worship
Pastor: God has established his kingdom, and invites each of us to be a part of it.

People: We do not understand everything about the Kingdom of God, but we do know it is a blessing we can experience.

Pastor: God increases his Kingdom as persons respond to the work of his Spirit.

People: We pray for God's Spirit to find responsive hearts, that his Kingdom may advance throughout the earth.

Collect
Almighty God, who increases your Kingdom wherever hearts are responsive to the work of your Holy Spirit: Work in our midst, that the feeble attempts of your church may be multiplied into great advances for your Kingdom. We pray in Jesus' name. Amen.

Prayer of Confession
We are your church, O God, and we struggle to make your church great. How often we fail to recognize that your Kingdom will advance only when we commit our efforts to you rather than our own institution. Forgive us when we feel our labors are independent of what you are doing through your Holy Spirit. Guide us in the consecration of our efforts to support your Kingdom rather than struggle to build our organization. We pray through Christ our Lord. Amen.

Hymns
"Come, Thou Almighty King"
"Father Eternal, Ruler of Creation"
"Jesus Shall Reign"
"Lead On, O King Eternal"

PROPER 7
Sunday between June 19 and 25 inclusive
(If after Trinity Sunday)

First Lesson: 2 Samuel 5:1-12
Theme: David's kingdom established by God

Call to Worship
Pastor: The strength of our nation lies in our devotion to God.
People: We cannot build a government that will survive if God's will is ignored.
Pastor: God's purpose for all nations is to serve in the best interest to all people.
People: May our nation be truly "under God" and fulfill his purpose in our world.

Collect
Almighty God, who is the chief architect for society: Inspire the nations of this land with a passion for human rights; that our world may become a community in which oppression is removed, and freedom is a universal blessing. In Christ's name we pray. Amen.

Prayer of Confession
We are proud of our nation, Father, and thank you for the privilege of being citizens. But our pride often causes us to leave you out of the picture. Forgive us when we reject your guidance in our national and international concerns. Help us to build a nation that sees the world as one family in which we share your concern and compassion with all people. We pray through Christ our Lord. Amen.

Hymns
"God of Our Fathers"
"My Country, 'Tis of Thee"
"O Beautiful for Spacious Skies"
"This Is My Song"

PROPER 7
Sunday between June 19 and 25 inclusive
(If after Trinity Sunday)

Second Lesson: 2 Corinthians 5:18—6:2
Theme: We live for Christ who died for us

Call to Worship
Pastor: Our sinful nature compels us to live selfishly without concern for others.
People: But our love for Christ compels us to live not for ourselves, but for him.
Pastor: Amen! It is Christ who died for us, and was raised to life who now determines our lifestyle.
People: We are glad to be Christians, and want our lives to show that we live for Christ.

Collect
Gracious Father, whose Son died and was raised to life for our sake: Fill our hearts with committed love to him; that we may no longer live for ourselves, but for Christ our Savior, in whose name we pray. Amen.

Prayer of Confession
Life is a precious gift, Father, which you give to us. But we confess we become selfish with it, even with our knowledge of Christ's sacrifice on our behalf. Forgive us when we live to satisfy our desires, instead of living to please our Savior. Unite us with Christ, that we may experience a new creation of our total being. In his name we pray. Amen.

Hymns
"Have Thine Own Way, Lord"
"I Am Thine, O Lord"
"Just As I Am, Thine Own to Be"
"My Jesus, As Thou Wilt"

PROPER 7
Sunday between June 19 and 25 inclusive
(If after Trinity Sunday)

Gospel: Mark 4:35-41
Theme: Jesus stills the storm

Call to Worship

Leader: Life is not without its storms; but remember, our storms are not without our Savior!

People: We know fear, but we also know faith. And Christ has stood by us in our storms.

Leader: Our Lord has power to bring peace to our troubled souls, if only we trust him to be the Lord he is.

People: We know who Jesus is, and trust him to overcome any fear which would destroy our faith.

Collect

Almighty God, whose Son is in command of life and stills the tempests which would trouble our souls: Increase our faith in his divine authority, that life may not toss us about at the mercy of our fears. In our Savior's name we pray. Amen.

Prayer of Confession

Our Father, we confess that fear has left its mark on each of us. We desire faith, and many times feel strong. But our mortal nature seems to have an overpowering force, and we become troubled for fear that life would destroy us. Forgive us when our faith does not reveal the presence of Christ who is able to calm our anxiety. Undergird us with confidence in our Lord's presence, that we may be defended against all tribulation. We pray through Christ our Lord. Amen.

Hymns

"Be Not Dismayed"
"Peace, Perfect Peace"
"Thou Hidden Source of Calm Repose"
"When the Storms of Life Are Raging"

PROPER 8
Sunday between June 26 and July 2 inclusive

First Lesson: 2 Samuel 6:1-15
Theme: The Ark is brought to Jerusalem

Call to Worship

Pastor: When we come into the sanctuary, we feel the presence of God.
People: We know God is everywhere, but we feel especially close to him here.
Pastor: The altar helps us to sense the nearness of God, and undergrids our worship of him.
People: We know God is here, and offer ourselves in praise and devotion.

Collect

Eternal God, whose presence is always about us: Help us to make our hearts your altar; that we may live and serve in the awareness that you are in our midst. In our Savior's name we pray. Amen.

Prayer of Confession

We need your presence, Father, to guide, strengthen, and protect us. But sometimes we are afraid of your presence because of our unworthiness. Forgive us when we try to keep our distance, thinking we are safer. Come into our lives and bless us with your grace and power; and give us your peace. In the name of Christ, we pray. Amen.

Hymns

"I Need Thee Every Hour"
"Nearer My God to Thee"
"O For a Closer Walk with God"
"When the Storms of Life Are Raging"

PROPER 8
Sunday between June 26 and July 2 inclusive

Second Lesson: 2 Corinthians 8:7-15
Theme: Christian stewardship of money

Call to Worship
Pastor: We measure wealth in terms of money. But our greatest wealth is the salvation Christ gives to us.
People: We are wealthy, spiritually, because Christ was willing to make himself poor on our behalf.
Pastor: That is why material wealth is a sacred trust. We give for the sake of others as Christ gave for our sake.
People: May the love of Christ flow through his church as we take seriously the needs of others.

Collect
Benevolent Father, whose Son became poor that we might become rich: Move us with genuine compassion to give freely of our wealth, that your church may be effective in its ministry to lift others out of spiritual poverty. We pray through Christ our Redeemer. Amen.

Prayer of Confession
We are wealthy people, Father, who prefer to complain about our debts rather than rejoice in your benevolence. Forgive us for selfishness which makes us ask of you in our prayers, but say no to others with our contributions. Give us a desire to support your church financially, not because of church bills, but because of the great gift you have given in Christ Jesus our Savior, through whom we pray. Amen.

Hymns
"As Men of God Their First Fruits Brought"
"I Gave My Life for Thee"
"More Love to Thee"
"We Give Thee But Thine Own"

PROPER 8
Sunday between June 26 and July 2 inclusive

Gospel: Mark 5:21-43
Theme: Miracles which illustrate salvation

Call to Worship

Leader: Sin appears to have power over us through the reality of death.
People: Death is real, but not final, because Christ our Savior has even greater power!
Leader: Christ is redemptive! All of us can experience the miracle of salvation and the miracle of life after death!
People: We know Christ is our Savior! We thank God for the faith he has placed within our hearts!

Collect

Gracious heavenly Father, who redeems our lives from the power of sin and death through your Son Jesus: Touch our lives with the healing of our souls; that we may be assured of our victory over sin and the grave to live victoriously with Christ our Redeemer, in whose name we pray. Amen.

Prayer of Confession

We want to be made whole, Father, assured that our sins are forgiven and our lives secure in your love. But sin makes us deny our devotion, and we feel unsure of our eternal destiny. Forgive us when we are insincere in our commitment, and sacrilegious with our lifestyles. Redeem us from the grip of sin; that we may be free to live a new life for you, made whole by the healing touch of Christ our Savior, through whom we pray. Amen.

Hymns

"Amazing Grace"
"Jesus, Thy Blood and Righteousness"
"O For a Thousand Tongues to Sing"
"Pass Me Not, O Gentle Savior"

PROPER 9
Sunday between July 3 and 9 inclusive

First Lesson: 2 Samuel 7:1-17
Theme: God's providence

Call to Worship
Pastor: In all of life, there is nothing so wonderful as God's providence.
People: God is so good. He guides, protects, provides, strengthens, loves, and forgives!
Pastor: We could go on and on, and never exhaust all the wonderful things God does for us.
People: We give thanks to God for caring so much for us.

Collect
Almighty God, whose main concern is the welfare of your people: May our praise and thanksgiving be as unending as your daily blessings that go on without end from one generation to the next. It is through Christ that we give you our praise. Amen.

Prayer of Confession
Eternal God, you are forever caring for us as a father cares for his children! Forgive us when we take such love for granted without responding with praise and thanksgiving. Accept our offerings of praise now; and keep us ever mindful of your blessings, and vocal in our appreciation. In the name of Christ we pray. Amen.

Hymns
"God of Our Life"
"Now Thank We All Our God"
"Praise to the Lord, the Almighty"
"We Come unto Our Fathers' God"

PROPER 9
Sunday between July 3 and 9 inclusive

Second Lesson: 2 Corinthians 12:1-10
Theme: In weakness we experience Christ's strength

Call to Worship
Pastor: We each have our own weakness, but that does not need to hinder our discipleship.
People: **We have felt inadequate, inferior, and quite worthless at times. And yet we know the joy of Christian discipleship.**
Pastor: If we could boast of our own strength, we would hinder Christ working through us, and little would be accomplished.
People: **Our strength is in Christ who uses us in spite of our weaknesses. We are glad to give him the glory!**

Collect
Eternal God, whose Son is the strength of your church, and who accomplishes much in spite of our human limitations: Make us alive and effective in our ministry, strengthened by the presence of Christ, that we may not hinder the growth of your church by our inabilities. We pray through Christ our Lord. Amen.

Prayer of Confession
There are so many things we cannot do well, Father, and we tend to give up. Sometimes we are proud of our abilities, and feel we have succeeded on our own strength. Forgive us when we have hurt the ministry of your church by not letting Christ be our strength. Take our inadequacies, and prove your power through a living vital church, committed to our Lord Jesus Christ, through whom we pray. Amen.

Hymns
"Christ is Made the Sure Foundation"
"God Is My Strong Salvation"
"Jesus My Strength, My Hope"
"The Church's One Foundation"

PROPER 9
Sunday between July 3 and 9 inclusive

Gospel: Mark 6:1-6
Theme: Jesus rejected in Nazareth

Call to Worship
Pastor: God's love and redeeming grace is great enough to save the worst sinner.
People: We believe that. But we also know God's love can be rejected, and salvation does not happen.
Pastor: Jesus experienced that in Nazareth. They were without faith, and Jesus could not help them.
People: May Jesus find us firm in our faith so he can transform our lives by his saving grace.

Collect
Gracious Father, whose Son was rejected by those who saw only his humanity and not his divinity, making their salvation hopeless: Open our hearts to the healing ministry of our Savior, that he may save us from the power of sin and death. In his name we pray. Amen.

Prayer of Confession
How often you are in our presence, Father, and our indifference keeps us from receiving the miracle of your forgiving grace! We take you for granted, because we have heard about you all our life. Forgive us when we refuse to listen to your word, or to be touched by your love. Renew our faith in Christ, that we may be ready and willing to have him restore us to new life. In his name we pray. Amen.

Hymns
"Come, Ye That Love the Lord"
"Draw Thou My Soul, O Christ"
"Have Thine Own Way"
"My Faith Looks Up to Thee"

PROPER 10
Sunday between July 10 and 16 inclusive

First Lesson: 2 Samuel 7:18-29
Theme: David's prayer of thanksgiving

CALL TO WORSHIP
Pastor: God is faithful to his people. We worship him alone as our God.
People: God has promised to bless us, and indeed he has!
Pastor: Let us come before God with prayers of thanksgiving.
People: Thanks be to you, O God, for making such wonderful promises to us; for keeping these promises; and for blessing us beyond your promises!

Collect
Almighty God, our benevolent Father: We are so unworthy of all that you do for us, and yet you continue to pour out your blessings on us. You are our God, and you alone we worship. We thank you with our total being for all that you are, and for all you have made us to be. We praise you through Christ our Lord. Amen.

Prayer of Confession
Were we to pray every minute, Father, we could not thank you enough for all your goodness. But more important, our thankfulness ought to show in our daily lives. Forgive us when we do not let our thankfulness show in the way we choose to live. Guide us into a life style that will give evidence to the thankfulness we feel in our hearts. In Jesus' name we pray. Amen.

Hymns
"Amazing Grace! How Sweet the Sound"
"How Great Thou Art"
"Standing on the Promises"
" 'Tis So Sweet to Trust in Jesus"

PROPER 10
Sunday between July 10 and 16 inclusive

Second Lesson: Ephesians 1:1-10
Theme: Brought to God by Christ

Call to Worship
Leader: God has made us his children through our faith in Jesus Christ!
People: Marvelous grace of Jesus! He saves us from sin to be God's children!
Leader: Jesus died on the cross to set us free. It is his desire that all accept his forgiveness.
People: We praise God for his love expressed in Jesus our Savior, and for the freedom he gives us!

Collect
Most gracious Father, who has chosen us to be your children through the love Christ expressed on our behalf: Unite us with our Savior by faith, that we may be set free from sin to live as your children. In Jesus' name we pray. Amen.

Prayer of Confession
We believe your desire is to make us your children, Father. But sin makes us strive for independence, and we are not free to be the people you have made us to be. Forgive us for our sins which keep us from living as your children. Fill our hearts with the love of Christ cleansing us from within, that we may give true praise for you being our Father. In the name of Christ we pray. Amen.

Hymns
"All Praise to Our Redeeming Lord"
"How Great Thou Art"
"I've Found A Friend"
"O Happy Day, That Fixed My Choice"

PROPER 10
Sunday between July 10 and 16 inclusive

Gospel: Mark 6:7-13
Theme: The twelve sent out two-by-two

Call to Worship
Pastor: We are messengers to our world in mission for our Lord Jesus Christ.
People: We carry the love of Christ in our hearts, and desire to share it with our world in his ministry.
Pastor: Christ has made us responsible for getting his message to as many as we can as quickly as we can.
People: May our Lord impress upon us the urgency to tell others about him.

Collect
Father in heaven, whose Son has given us the message of your love to share with our world: Equip us for Christian ministry as our Lord's disciples, that our witness may convince others to turn from their sins. In our Savior's name we pray. Amen.

Prayer of Confession
The mission of your church is vital to our world, Father. But our concept of being in mission is more in terms of service and meetings to go to, than it is in sharing our faith with those who may reject our witness. Forgive our hesitancy to tell the story of Jesus. Send us forth with a definite goal of winning others to Christ as Lord and Savior, in whose name we pray. Amen.

Hymns
"I Love to Tell the Story"
"O Zion, Haste"
"The Voice of God Is Calling"
"We've A Story to Tell to the Nations"

PROPER 11
Sunday between July 17 and 23 inclusive

First Lesson: 2 Samuel 11:1-15
Theme: Tragedy and triumph in the life of David

Call to Worship
Pastor: We cannot help admiring King David for his great leadership among the Israelites.
People: Would that we had more leaders like him today!
Pastor: David had to face the reality of sin and sorrow in his life like all of us; but he became great because of what he let God do through him.
People: May God find us receptive to his will in our lives.

Collect
Loving Father, whose creative redemption is able to make strong saints out of weak sinners: Receive us with our imperfections, and remake us to be strong in your power. May our past sins in life make us all the more aware of our dependence on you. We pray through Christ our Lord. Amen.

Prayer of Confession
Father in heaven, we come in confession of our sins. Not only have we sinned, but we have even ignored the guilt of our sins. We have also hampered our ability to serve in your name because of our human frailties. Forgive us for accepting these limitations as reasons for not being what you want us to be. Assure us of your forgiveness, and then encourage us with your Spirit to be victorious in the challenges life presents.

Hymns
"Fight the Good Fight"
"Have Thine Own Way"
"My Soul, Be on Thy Guard"
"Once to Every Man and Nation"

PROPER 11
Sunday between July 17 and 23 inclusive

Second Lesson: Ephesians 2:11-22
Theme: Unity in Christ

Call to Worship
Pastor: Jesus died on the cross as Savior of the world.
People: His sacrifice destroys all barriers which divide God's family.
Pastor: Our divisions are based on sin. But Jesus brings us together as brothers and sisters to worship God in Christian love.
People: We rejoice in the peace which Christ gives to those who serve him as Lord and Savior!

Collect
O God, our heavenly Father, who unites us as one family by the sacrificial death of your Son: Fill our hearts with genuine love toward all people, that our prejudices may not destroy the unity of spirit which Christ our Lord has provided. In his name we pray. Amen.

Prayer of Confession
Love is so limited for us, Father. We exclude more people than we include when we are honest with our feelings of love. Forgive us for maintaining our prejudices which Christ destroyed with his death on the cross. Teach us to live as brothers and sisters who love one another, and who have learned how to cross over the barriers which once separated us. In our Savior's name we pray. Amen.

Hymns
"Blest Be the Dear Uniting Love"
"In Christ There Is No East or West"
"Jesus, United by Thy Grace"
"We Are One in the Spirit"

PROPER 11
Sunday between July 17 and 23 inclusive

Gospel: Mark 6:30-44
Theme: Jesus' compassion

Call to Worship
Leader: Jesus demonstrated his pastoral concern when he saw crowds who were like sheep without a shepherd.
People: Even though he was tired and wanted to be alone, Jesus gave himself to those who needed his ministry.
Leader: Jesus continues his pastoral ministry today through the church as it reaches out to those in need.
People: May we have the same compassion our Lord expressed as we minister in his name.

Collect
Heavenly Father, whose Son gave himself to others out of a genuine concern for their needs: Inspire your church today with that same compassion, that we may share your word and redemption with those who feel life has left them empty. In our Savior's name we pray. Amen.

Prayer of Confession
We feel grateful, Father, when we read in your word the sincere compassion of our Lord. But we fail to realize that our Lord needs his church to be the instrument of his compassion to our world today. Forgive us when we ignore the crowds who have spiritual needs which our Lord is able to help. Grant us genuine concern which will enable us to fulfill our ministry with compassion. We pray through Christ our Lord. Amen.

Hymns
"O Brother Man, Fold to Thy Heart"
"O Thou Who Art the Shepherd"
"The Voice of God Is Calling"
"Where Cross the Crowded Ways of Life"

PROPER 12
Sunday between July 24 and 30 inclusive

First Lesson: 2 Samuel 12:1-14
Theme: Confronted by God with our sin

Call to Worship
Pastor: Sinful as we are, God invites us to come to him.
People: It is difficult to come into the Lord's presence when we are guilty of sin.
Pastor: If we are willing to come to God in confession; God is willing to come to us in forgiveness.
People: We know we are sinners. We come in the assurance that God accepts us, and forgives our sins.

Collect
Most merciful Father, whose nature it is to forgive the sins of the penitent: Free us from our fear to come to you in confession; that we may experience your cleansing and blessing of a new beginning. In our Savior's name we pray. Amen.

Prayer of Confession
We do not presume to hide our sins, Father, but we do avoid talking to you about them. Forgive us not only for our sins of disobedience, but for not coming in faith to receive your forgiveness. Cleanse us of our unrighteousness; and lead us in a closer relationship with you. In Jesus' name we pray. Amen.

Hymns
"Come Every Soul by Sin Oppressed"
"I Am Coming to the Cross"
"I Heard the Voice of Jesus Say"
"Jesus Is Tenderly Calling"

PROPER 12
Sunday between July 24 and 30 inclusive

Second Lesson: Ephesians 3:14-21
Theme: The love of Christ

Call to Worship
Pastor: God has revealed his love to us through his Son, Jesus Christ.
People: We believe in that love; and we have faith in Christ to share it with us.
Pastor: His love is always available. But to experience it, we must invite Christ into our hearts.
People: May Christ come with his gift of love, and enable us to share it with others.

Collect
Gracious God, who shares your love with us through your Son: Give us the power to resist the sinful nature of our old being; that we may become new persons in Christ, reborn to live a new life in thanksgiving for your love. In our Savior's name we pray. Amen.

Prayer of Confession
We want to be Christians, Father, because we believe that is the right way to live. But it is difficult for us to give up our sinful ways in order to be the Christians our Lord calls us to be. Forgive us when we deny your love, and continue in our sins. Deepen our faith and our commitment; that we may respond to your love and live as persons whom Christ has redeemed. In his name we pray. Amen.

Hymns
"Love Divine, All Loves Excelling"
"I Love to Tell the Story"
"I've Found a Friend"
"Lord Jesus, I Love Thee"

PROPER 12
Sunday between July 24 and 30 inclusive

Gospel: John 6:1-15
Theme: Jesus feeds five thousand men

Call to Worship
Pastor: Our Savior is a compassionate Lord, who is willing and able to feed our hungry souls.
People: We worship our Lord, knowing he will feed us the bread of life as we open our hearts to him.
Pastor: You who are hungry, come with the assurance that you will be fed. For Christ is in our midst to nourish our souls.
People: We come, believing our hunger shall be satisfied, and rejoicing in our privilege to be fed by Christ!

Collect
Gracious Father, whose Son knows our spiritual hunger, and feeds us the bread of life: Help us to open our hearts completely to his word; that we may hear, understand, and receive the nourishment he gives to our souls. In his name we pray. Amen.

Prayer of Confession
We feel empty at times, Father, as if our souls were depleted of all strength. We wonder where to turn when all our materialistic endeavors leave us starved. Forgive us for trying to satisfy our spiritual hunger with the false food of sinful pleasure and selfish gain. Feed us with the love of Christ, filling our hearts with the joy of forgiveness and the hope of new life. We pray through Christ our Lord. Amen.

Hymns
"All the Way My Savior Leads Me"
"Break Thou the Bread of Life"
"Come, Ye Disconsolate"
"I Need Thee Every Hour"

PROPER 13
Sunday between July 31 and August 6 inclusive

First Lesson: 2 Samuel 12:15b-24
Theme: David's infant son dies

Call to Worship
Pastor: We worship God today, aware that our love relationships must some day be broken by death.
People: Such separation is very painful for us to accept, but we know death is not the end of life.
Pastor: That is why we are able to accept the reality of death. We know God has something better in store.
People: We thank God for sharing his immortality with us that gives us victory over death!

Collect
Eternal God, who knows how we suffer when a loved one dies: Grant us faith to see beyond our pain, with the assurance that death is a transition into a fuller life. Thus may our sorrow be turned into joy in celebration of our immortality. We pray through Christ, or risen Lord. Amen.

Prayer of Confession
Our faith is in your Son, O God, who has shown us our victory over death. But we confess that our pain in losing loved ones often clouds over our faith; and our pain is more severe. Forgive us, not for hurting, but for not sharing our hurt with you, so we can be comforted. Give us courage to face what cannot be changed in this life, in the full confidence that we are eternally in your care. In our Savior's name we pray. Amen.

Hymns
"For All the Saints"
"Give Me the Wings of Faith"
"I Know Not What the Future Hath"
"Servant of God, Well Done"

PROPER 13
Sunday between July 31 and August 6 inclusive

Second Lesson: Ephesians 4:1-6
Theme: Unity in the church

Call to Worship

Leader: There is one Christ, therefore one church, but with many different responsibilities.

People: God has made us to be different people, but with one faith to serve our Lord.

Leader: We celebrate our unity in Christ, and our diversity in ministry, that all kinds of people may be brought into our Lord's saving grace!

People: Praise God for the many different gifts with which he has endowed his church, united as the body of Christ!

Collect

Heavenly Father, who brings together our many different forms of ministry into one church with the mission to proclaim our Lord's salvation: Unite us by our faith in Christ as one church, that our individual commitments of time and talent may contribute to the total ministry of your church. We pray through Christ our Lord. Amen.

Prayer of Confession

Christ has called us into ministry, Father, to be his church in our world. But we hinder that ministry when we let our different forms of ministry separate us from one another. Forgive us for the fractured body of Christ through which we try to witness to our world. Give us unity of spirit, that we may be a united church, leading our world to Christ. In his name we pray. Amen.

Hymns

"All Praise to Our Redeeming Lord"
"Break Forth, O Living Light of God"
"Christ Is Made the Sure Foundation"
"The Church's One Foundation"

PROPER 13
Sunday between July 31 and August 6 inclusive

Gospel: John 6:24-35
Theme: The Bread of Life

Call to Worship
Pastor: Blessed are those who hunger for Jesus to feed their souls.
People: Jesus is the Bread of Life who satisfies the heart's deepest desire.
Pastor: He comes to us from God to feed us with our Father's love, and nurture our spiritual growth.
People: We feed on our Savior's love, desiring to grow in his likeness.

Collect
Eternal God, who has sent your only-begotten Son to feed our souls with your truth and grace: Come to us in this moment of worship; that as we hunger for righteousness, we may be satisfied by the Bread of Life, through whom we pray. Amen.

Prayer of Confession
We confess to you, Father, that our worship is often the cry of hunger. We feel pain in our hearts because we are guilty of sin and want to be forgiven. We choose sin, and empty our lives of joy, peace, and happiness. And our hunger becomes even more severe. Cleanse us of our unrighteousness, and feed us your truth; that we may have our souls satisfied for eternity. In our Savior's name we pray. Amen.

Hymns
"Blessed Jesus, at Thy Word"
"Break Thou the Bread of Life"
"Guide Me, O Thou Great Jehovah"
"Just as I Am, Without One Plea"

PROPER 14
Sunday between August 7 and 13 inclusive

First Lesson: 2 Samuel 18:1, 5, 9-15
Theme: Death of Absalom

Call to Worship

Leader: History is God telling "his story" of love and peace.
People: Our history seems to be a history of war more than peace.
Leader: That is what happens when we interfere with God's story. War instead of peace is a constant struggle God has with his people.
People: May we do our best to help God have his way, so "his story" will be one of peace for all people.

Collect

Heavenly Father, who wills that we live in peace with one another: Remove all causes of greed and fear, hatred and prejudice; that we may look for ways to strengthen our family ties with people of all nations. In the name of Christ we pray. Amen.

Prayer of Confession

We know whenever there is war, Father, that all society suffers. Yet we continue to harbor feelings against others which lead to war. Forgive us for that which motivates us to destroy our sisters and brothers. Inspire us to bring into being a world that not only respects human life, but also protects it from self-destruction. Hear us for Jesus' sake. Amen.

Hymns

"God of Our Fathers"
"Hope of the World"
"Once to Every Man and Nation"
"This Is My Song"

PROPER 14
Sunday between August 7 and 13 inclusive

Second Lesson: Ephesians 4:25 — 5:2
Theme: Love as Christ loved us

Call to Worship
Pastor: God has marked us as his by giving us his Holy Spirit.
People: **It is God's Spirit who enables us to live the Christian life.**
Pastor: It is God's Spirit who helps us to love one another as Christ loves us.
People: **We pray that our lives will not grieve the Holy Spirit with bitterness or strife, but be examples of his love and forgiveness.**

Collect
O God our heavenly Father, who gives your love and forgiveness to us through your Son Jesus: Touch our lives with your Holy Spirit, that we may prove we belong to you by sharing a life which reveals our Savior's love. In his name we pray. Amen.

Prayer of Confession
We are grateful for our Savior's love, Father, and pray that we may be controlled by that same love. Forgive us when we give in to bitterness and unkind feelings toward others. Fill us with your Spirit; that we may sincerely love and forgive one another in the same way that we are loved and forgiven by Christ our Savior, through whom we pray. Amen.

Hymns
"At Length There Dawns the Glorious Day"
"Blest Be the Tie That Binds"
"O Brother Man, Fold to Thy Heart"
"O Spirit of the Living God"

PROPER 14
Sunday between August 7 and 13 inclusive

Gospel: John 6:35, 41-51
Theme: Jesus, our source of eternal life

Call to Worship

Pastor: God our Father leads us by his Spirit to receive his Son Jesus as our Savior.
People: We believe Jesus is God's Son who has taught us the truth of God's love.
Pastor: By faith, we believe Jesus died for us and arose, opening the door to eternal life.
People: We come to Jesus believing he will feed us with God's love, and give us eternal life.

Collect

Gracious Father, who inspires us with faith in your Son, thereby granting us the hope of eternal life: Feed our souls with your truth and love as we worship your Son, that we may have the assurance of eternal life with you. We pray through Christ our Lord. Amen.

Prayer of Confession

Father, we feel you prompting our spirits to receive Jesus as our Lord and Savior. But we confess we often act as if we believe he is the Savior of the world, but not our Savior. Forgive us when we avoid his invitation to partake of the living bread which came from heaven. Give us open and receptive hearts to his gift of life which continues forever. In our Savior's name we pray. Amen.

Hymns

"Come, Sinners to the Gospel Feast"
"Guide Me, O Thou Great Jehovah"
"O Son of God Incarnate"
"Spirit of Faith, Come Down"

PROPER 15
Sunday between August 14 and 20 inclusive

First Lesson: 2 Samuel 18:24-33
Theme: David mourns Absalom

Call to Worship
Pastor: Grief is a difficult pain to deal with, because it cuts so deep into our hearts.
People: It is like a heavy burden with more weight than we can bear.
Pastor: But it is not too heavy for our Lord, who is able to help us in our grief.
People: Thanks be to God, who shares our grief, convincing us we can believe in his healing and recovery.

Collect
Father in heaven, who eases the burden of the grieving heart through the comfort of your Holy Spirit: In our hour of grief, be our strength and support; that we may be able to endure, and have reason to rejoice in your goodness. In our Savior's name we pray. Amen.

Prayer of Confession
Grief is like a curse to the human race, Father, because it is so painful. Yet we know we cannot avoid it; and we also know strength can come from it. Forgive us when we succumb to its misery, instead of turning to you for support. Draw us close to you; that in our grief we may feel your defense. We pray in Jesus' name. Amen.

Hymns
"Be Not Dismayed"
"Be Still, My Soul"
"Come, Ye Disconsolate"
"Thou Hidden Source of Calm Repose"

PROPER 15
Sunday between August 14 and 20 inclusive

Second Lesson: Ephesians 5:15-20
Theme: Be careful how you live

Call to Worship
Leader: Every day God blesses us with new opportunities to live for him!
People: We thank God for the gift of life, and the joy he allows us to experience.
Leader: God challenges us to make good use of each day, so that evil does not have a chance to mislead us.
People: We trust God to lead us each day according to his will, so that we may please him with our lives.

Collect
Gracious Father, who enables us with your Spirit to live the Christian life: Lead us in a life of Christian fellowship, love, and service, that we may take advantage of the opportunities you give us to enjoy life at its fullest. In the name of Christ we pray. Amen.

Prayer of Confession
We want to live as Christians, Father, but our human nature makes it difficult for us to follow your Spirit. Forgive us when we follow the world's example instead of being an example to the world. Let our thoughts, speech, and behavior contribute to the spiritual nurture of your people. We pray through Christ our Lord. Amen.

Hymns
"Breathe on Me, Breath of God"
"Holy Spirit, Truth Divine"
"Spirit of God, Descend upon my Heart"
"Take My Life, and Let It Be Consecrated"

PROPER 15
Sunday between August 14 and 20 inclusive

Second Lesson: Ephesians 5:15-20
Theme: Be careful how you live

Call to Worship

Leader: Every day God blesses us with new opportunities to live for him!

People: **We thank God for the gift of life, and the joy he allows us to experience.**

Leader: God challenges us to make good use of each day, so that evil does not have a chance to mislead us.

People: **We trust God to lead us each day according to his will, so that we may please him with our lives.**

Collect

Gracious Father, who enables us with your Spirit to live the Christian life: Lead us in a life of Christian fellowship, love, and service, that we may take advantage of the opportunities you give us to enjoy life at its fullest. In the name of Christ we pray. Amen.

Prayer of Confession

We want to live as Christians, Father, but our human nature makes it difficult for us to follow your Spirit. Forgive us when we follow the world's example instead of being an example to the world. Let our thoughts, speech, and behavior contribute to the spiritual nurture of your people. We pray through Christ our Lord. Amen.

Hymns

"Breathe on Me, Breath of God"
"Holy Spirit, Truth Divine"
"Spirit of God, Descend upon my Heart"
"Take My Life, and Let It Be Consecrated"

PROPER 15
Sunday between August 14 and 20 inclusive

First Lesson: 2 Samuel 18:24-33
Theme: David mourns Absalom

Call to Worship
Pastor: Grief is a difficult pain to deal with, because it cuts so deep into our hearts.
People: **It is like a heavy burden with more weight than we can bear.**
Pastor: But it is not too heavy for our Lord, who is able to help us in our grief.
People: **Thanks be to God, who shares our grief, convincing us we can believe in his healing and recovery.**

Collect
Father in heaven, who eases the burden of the grieving heart through the comfort of your Holy Spirit: In our hour of grief, be our strength and support; that we may be able to endure, and have reason to rejoice in your goodness. In our Savior's name we pray. Amen.

Prayer of Confession
Grief is like a curse to the human race, Father, because it is so painful. Yet we know we cannot avoid it; and we also know strength can come from it. Forgive us when we succumb to its misery, instead of turning to you for support. Draw us close to you; that in our grief we may feel your defense. We pray in Jesus' name. Amen.

Hymns
"Be Not Dismayed"
"Be Still, My Soul"
"Come, Ye Disconsolate"
"Thou Hidden Source of Calm Repose"

PROPER 14
Sunday between August 7 and 13 inclusive

Gospel: John 6:35, 41-51
Theme: Jesus, our source of eternal life

Call to Worship
Pastor: God our Father leads us by his Spirit to receive his Son Jesus as our Savior.
People: We believe Jesus is God's Son who has taught us the truth of God's love.
Pastor: By faith, we believe Jesus died for us and arose, opening the door to eternal life.
People: We come to Jesus believing he will feed us with God's love, and give us eternal life.

Collect
Gracious Father, who inspires us with faith in your Son, thereby granting us the hope of eternal life: Feed our souls with your truth and love as we worship your Son, that we may have the assurance of eternal life with you. We pray through Christ our Lord. Amen.

Prayer of Confession
Father, we feel you prompting our spirits to receive Jesus as our Lord and Savior. But we confess we often act as if we believe he is the Savior of the world, but not our Savior. Forgive us when we avoid his invitation to partake of the living bread which came from heaven. Give us open and receptive hearts to his gift of life which continues forever. In our Savior's name we pray. Amen.

Hymns
"Come, Sinners to the Gospel Feast"
"Guide Me, O Thou Great Jehovah"
"O Son of God Incarnate"
"Spirit of Faith, Come Down"

PROPER 14
Sunday between August 7 and 13 inclusive

Second Lesson: Ephesians 4:25 — 5:2
Theme: Love as Christ loved us

Call to Worship
Pastor: God has marked us as his by giving us his Holy Spirit.
People: It is God's Spirit who enables us to live the Christian life.
Pastor: It is God's Spirit who helps us to love one another as Christ loves us.
People: We pray that our lives will not grieve the Holy Spirit with bitterness or strife, but be examples of his love and forgiveness.

Collect
O God our heavenly Father, who gives your love and forgiveness to us through your Son Jesus: Touch our lives with your Holy Spirit, that we may prove we belong to you by sharing a life which reveals our Savior's love. In his name we pray. Amen.

Prayer of Confession
We are grateful for our Savior's love, Father, and pray that we may be controlled by that same love. Forgive us when we give in to bitterness and unkind feelings toward others. Fill us with your Spirit; that we may sincerely love and forgive one another in the same way that we are loved and forgiven by Christ our Savior, through whom we pray. Amen.

Hymns
"At Length There Dawns the Glorious Day"
"Blest Be the Tie That Binds"
"O Brother Man, Fold to Thy Heart"
"O Spirit of the Living God"

PROPER 14
Sunday between August 7 and 13 inclusive

First Lesson: 2 Samuel 18:1, 5, 9-15
Theme: Death of Absalom

Call to Worship
Pastor: History is God telling "his story" of love and peace.
People: Our history seems to be a history of war more than peace.
Pastor: That is what happens when we interfere with God's story. War instead of peace is a constant struggle God has with his people.
People: May we do our best to help God have his way, so "his story" will be one of peace for all people.

Collect
Heavenly Father, who wills that we live in peace with one another: Remove all causes of greed and fear, hatred and prejudice; that we may look for ways to strengthen our family ties with people of all nations. In the name of Christ we pray. Amen.

Prayer of Confession
We know whenever there is war, Father, that all society suffers. Yet we continue to harbor feelings against others which lead to war. Forgive us for that which motivates us to destroy our sisters and brothers. Inspire us to bring into being a world that not only respects human life, but also protects it from self-destruction. Hear us for Jesus' sake. Amen.

Hymns
"God of Our Fathers"
"Hope of the World"
"Once to Every Man and Nation"
"This Is My Song"

PROPER 13
Sunday between July 31 and August 6 inclusive

Gospel: John 6:24-35
Theme: The Bread of Life

Call to Worship
Pastor: Blessed are those who hunger for Jesus to feed their souls.
People: Jesus is the Bread of Life who satisfies the heart's deepest desire.
Pastor: He comes to us from God to feed us with our Father's love, and nurture our spiritual growth.
People: We feed on our Savior's love, desiring to grow in his likeness.

Collect
Eternal God, who has sent your only-begotten Son to feed our souls with your truth and grace: Come to us in this moment of worship; that as we hunger for righteousness, we may be satisfied by the Bread of Life, through whom we pray. Amen.

Prayer of Confession
We confess to you, Father, that our worship is often the cry of hunger. We feel pain in our hearts because we are guilty of sin and want to be forgiven. We choose sin, and empty our lives of joy, peace, and happiness. And our hunger becomes even more severe. Cleanse us of our unrighteousness, and feed us your truth; that we may have our souls satisfied for eternity. In our Savior's name we pray. Amen.

Hymns
"Blessed Jesus, at Thy Word"
"Break Thou the Bread of Life"
"Guide Me, O Thou Great Jehovah"
"Just as I Am, Without One Plea"

PROPER 13
Sunday between July 31 and August 6 inclusive

Second Lesson: Ephesians 4:1-6
Theme: Unity in the church

Call to Worship
Pastor: There is one Christ, therefore one church, but with many different responsibilities.
People: God has made us to be different people, but with one faith to serve our Lord.
Pastor: We celebrate our unity in Christ, and our diversity in ministry, that all kinds of people may be brought into our Lord's saving grace!
People: Praise God for the many different gifts with which he has endowed his church, united as the body of Christ!

Collect
Heavenly Father, who brings together our many different forms of ministry into one church with the mission to proclaim our Lord's salvation: Unite us by our faith in Christ as one church, that our individual commitments of time and talent may contribute to the total ministry of your church. We pray through Christ our Lord. Amen.

Prayer of Confession
Christ has called us into ministry, Father, to be his church in our world. But we hinder that ministry when we let our different forms of ministry separate us from one another. Forgive us for the fractured body of Christ through which we try to witness to our world. Give us unity of spirit, that we may be a united church, leading our world to Christ. In his name we pray. Amen.

Hymns
"All Praise to Our Redeeming Lord"
"Break Forth, O Living Light of God"
"Christ Is Made the Sure Foundation"
"The Church's One Foundation"

PROPER 13
Sunday between July 31 and August 6 inclusive

First Lesson: 2 Samuel 12:15b-24
Theme: David's infant son dies

Call to Worship
Pastor: We worship God today, aware that our love relationships must some day be broken by death.
People: Such separation is very painful for us to accept, but we know death is not the end of life.
Pastor: That is why we are able to accept the reality of death. We know God has something better in store.
People: We thank God for sharing his immortality with us that gives us victory over death!

Collect
Eternal God, who knows how we suffer when a loved one dies: Grant us faith to see beyond our pain, with the assurance that death is a transition into a fuller life. Thus may our sorrow be turned into joy in celebration of our immortality. We pray through Christ, or risen Lord. Amen.

Prayer of Confession
Our faith is in your Son, O God, who has shown us our victory over death. But we confess that our pain in losing loved ones often clouds over our faith; and our pain is more severe. Forgive us, not for hurting, but for not sharing our hurt with you, so we can be comforted. Give us courage to face what cannot be changed in this life, in the full confidence that we are eternally in your care. In our Savior's name we pray. Amen.

Hymns
"For All the Saints"
"Give Me the Wings of Faith"
"I Know Not What the Future Hath"
"Servant of God, Well Done"

PROPER 12
Sunday between July 24 and 30 inclusive

Gospel: John 6:1-15
Theme: Jesus feeds five thousand men

Call to Worship
Pastor: Our Savior is a compassionate Lord, who is willing and able to feed our hungry souls.
People: We worship our Lord, knowing he will feed us the bread of life as we open our hearts to him.
Pastor: You who are hungry, come with the assurance that you will be fed. For Christ is in our midst to nourish our souls.
People: We come, believing our hunger shall be satisfied, and rejoicing in our privilege to be fed by Christ!

Collect
Gracious Father, whose Son knows our spiritual hunger, and feeds us the bread of life: Help us to open our hearts completely to his word; that we may hear, understand, and receive the nourishment he gives to our souls. In his name we pray. Amen.

Prayer of Confession
We feel empty at times, Father, as if our souls were depleted of all strength. We wonder where to turn when all our materialistic endeavors leave us starved. Forgive us for trying to satisfy our spiritual hunger with the false food of sinful pleasure and selfish gain. Feed us with the love of Christ, filling our hearts with the joy of forgiveness and the hope of new life. We pray through Christ our Lord. Amen.

Hymns
"All the Way My Savior Leads Me"
"Break Thou the Bread of Life"
"Come, Ye Disconsolate"
"I Need Thee Every Hour"

PROPER 12
Sunday between July 24 and 30 inclusive

Second Lesson: Ephesians 3:14-21
Theme: The love of Christ

Call to Worship
Pastor: God has revealed his love to us through his Son, Jesus Christ.
People: We believe in that love; and we have faith in Christ to share it with us.
Pastor: His love is always available. But to experience it, we must invite Christ into our hearts.
People: May Christ come with his gift of love, and enable us to share it with others.

Collect
Gracious God, who shares your love with us through your Son: Give us the power to resist the sinful nature of our old being; that we may become new persons in Christ, reborn to live a new life in thanksgiving for your love. In our Savior's name we pray. Amen.

Prayer of Confession
We want to be Christians, Father, because we believe that is the right way to live. But it is difficult for us to give up our sinful ways in order to be the Christians our Lord calls us to be. Forgive us when we deny your love, and continue in our sins. Deepen our faith and our commitment; that we may respond to your love and live as persons whom Christ has redeemed. In his name we pray. Amen.

Hymns
"Love Divine, All Loves Excelling"
"I Love to Tell the Story"
"I've Found a Friend"
"Lord Jesus, I Love Thee"

PROPER 12
Sunday between July 24 and 30 inclusive

First Lesson: 2 Samuel 12:1-14
Theme: Confronted by God with our sin

Call to Worship
Pastor: Sinful as we are, God invites us to come to him.
People: It is difficult to come into the Lord's presence when we are guilty of sin.
Pastor: If we are willing to come to God in confession; God is willing to come to us in forgiveness.
People: We know we are sinners. We come in the assurance that God accepts us, and forgives our sins.

Collect
Most merciful Father, whose nature it is to forgive the sins of the penitent: Free us from our fear to come to you in confession; that we may experience your cleansing and blessing of a new beginning. In our Savior's name we pray. Amen.

Prayer of Confession
We do not presume to hide our sins, Father, but we do avoid talking to you about them. Forgive us not only for our sins of disobedience, but for not coming in faith to receive your forgiveness. Cleanse us of our unrighteousness; and lead us in a closer relationship with you. In Jesus' name we pray. Amen.

Hymns
"Come Every Soul by Sin Oppressed"
"I Am Coming to the Cross"
"I Heard the Voice of Jesus Say"
"Jesus Is Tenderly Calling"

PROPER 11
Sunday between July 17 and 23 inclusive

Gospel: Mark 6:30-44
Theme: Jesus' compassion

Call to Worship
Pastor: Jesus demonstrated his pastoral concern when he saw crowds who were like sheep without a shepherd.
People: Even though he was tired and wanted to be alone, Jesus gave himself to those who needed his ministry.
Pastor: Jesus continues his pastoral ministry today through the church as it reaches out to those in need.
People: May we have the same compassion our Lord expressed as we minister in his name.

Collect
Heavenly Father, whose Son gave himself to others out of a genuine concern for their needs: Inspire your church today with that same compassion, that we may share your word and redemption with those who feel life has left them empty. In our Savior's name we pray. Amen.

Prayer of Confession
We feel grateful, Father, when we read in your word the sincere compassion of our Lord. But we fail to realize that our Lord needs his church to be the instrument of his compassion to our world today. Forgive us when we ignore the crowds who have spiritual needs which our Lord is able to help. Grant us genuine concern which will enable us to fulfill our ministry with compassion. We pray through Christ our Lord. Amen.

Hymns
"O Brother Man, Fold to Thy Heart"
"O Thou Who Art the Shepherd"
"The Voice of God Is Calling"
"Where Cross the Crowded Ways of Life"

PROPER 11
Sunday between July 17 and 23 inclusive

Second Lesson: Ephesians 2:11-22
Theme: Unity in Christ

Call to Worship
Pastor: Jesus died on the cross as Savior of the world.
People: His sacrifice destroys all barriers which divide God's family.
Pastor: Our divisions are based on sin. But Jesus brings us together as brothers and sisters to worship God in Christian love.
People: We rejoice in the peace which Christ gives to those who serve him as Lord and Savior!

Collect
O God, our heavenly Father, who unites us as one family by the sacrificial death of your Son: Fill our hearts with genuine love toward all people, that our prejudices may not destroy the unity of spirit which Christ our Lord has provided. In his name we pray. Amen.

Prayer of Confession
Love is so limited for us, Father. We exclude more people than we include when we are honest with our feelings of love. Forgive us for maintaining our prejudices which Christ destroyed with his death on the cross. Teach us to live as brothers and sisters who love one another, and who have learned how to cross over the barriers which once separated us. In our Savior's name we pray. Amen.

Hymns
"Blest Be the Dear Uniting Love"
"In Christ There Is No East or West"
"Jesus, United by Thy Grace"
"We Are One in the Spirit"

PROPER 11
Sunday between July 17 and 23 inclusive

First Lesson: 2 Samuel 11:1-15
Theme: Tragedy and triumph in the life of David

Call to Worship
Pastor: We cannot help admiring King David for his great leadership among the Israelites.
People: Would that we had more leaders like him today!
Pastor: David had to face the reality of sin and sorrow in his life like all of us; but he became great because of what he let God do through him.
People: May God find us receptive to his will in our lives.

Collect
Loving Father, whose creative redemption is able to make strong saints out of weak sinners: Receive us with our imperfections, and remake us to be strong in your power. May our past sins in life make us all the more aware of our dependence on you. We pray through Christ our Lord. Amen.

Prayer of Confession
Father in heaven, we come in confession of our sins. Not only have we sinned, but we have even ignored the guilt of our sins. We have also hampered our ability to serve in your name because of our human frailties. Forgive us for accepting these limitations as reasons for not being what you want us to be. Assure us of your forgiveness, and then encourage us with your Spirit to be victorious in the challenges life presents.

Hymns
"Fight the Good Fight"
"Have Thine Own Way"
"My Soul, Be on Thy Guard"
"Once to Every Man and Nation"

PROPER 10
Sunday between July 10 and 16 inclusive

Gospel: Mark 6:7-13
Theme: The twelve sent out two-by-two

Call to Worship
Pastor: We are messengers to our world in mission for our Lord Jesus Christ.
People: We carry the love of Christ in our hearts, and desire to share it with our world in his ministry.
Pastor: Christ has made us responsible for getting his message to as many as we can as quickly as we can.
People: May our Lord impress upon us the urgency to tell others about him.

Collect
Father in heaven, whose Son has given us the message of your love to share with our world: Equip us for Christian ministry as our Lord's disciples, that our witness may convince others to turn from their sins. In our Savior's name we pray. Amen.

Prayer of Confession
The mission of your church is vital to our world, Father. But our concept of being in mission is more in terms of service and meetings to go to, than it is in sharing our faith with those who may reject our witness. Forgive our hesitancy to tell the story of Jesus. Send us forth with a definite goal of winning others to Christ as Lord and Savior, in whose name we pray. Amen.

Hymns
"I Love to Tell the Story"
"O Zion, Haste"
"The Voice of God Is Calling"
"We've A Story to Tell to the Nations"

PROPER 10
Sunday between July 10 and 16 inclusive

Second Lesson: Ephesians 1:1-10
Theme: Brought to God by Christ

Call to Worship
Leader: God has made us his children through our faith in Jesus Christ!
People: Marvelous grace of Jesus! He saves us from sin to be God's children!
Leader: Jesus died on the cross to set us free. It is his desire that all accept his forgiveness.
People: We praise God for his love expressed in Jesus our Savior, and for the freedom he gives us!

Collect
Most gracious Father, who has chosen us to be your children through the love Christ expressed on our behalf: Unite us with our Savior by faith, that we may be set free from sin to live as your children. In Jesus' name we pray. Amen.

Prayer of Confession
We believe your desire is to make us your children, Father. But sin makes us strive for independence, and we are not free to be the people you have made us to be. Forgive us for our sins which keep us from living as your children. Fill our hearts with the love of Christ cleansing us from within, that we may give true praise for you being our Father. In the name of Christ we pray. Amen.

Hymns
"All Praise to Our Redeeming Lord"
"How Great Thou Art"
"I've Found A Friend"
"O Happy Day, That Fixed My Choice"

PROPER 10
Sunday between July 10 and 16 inclusive

First Lesson: 2 Samuel 7:18-29
Theme: David's prayer of thanksgiving

CALL TO WORSHIP
Pastor: God is faithful to his people. We worship him alone as our God.
People: God has promised to bless us, and indeed he has!
Pastor: Let us come before God with prayers of thanksgiving.
People: Thanks be to you, O God, for making such wonderful promises to us; for keeping these promises; and for blessing us beyond your promises!

Collect
Almighty God, our benevolent Father: We are so unworthy of all that you do for us, and yet you continue to pour out your blessings on us. You are our God, and you alone we worship. We thank you with our total being for all that you are, and for all you have made us to be. We praise you through Christ our Lord. Amen.

Prayer of Confession
Were we to pray every minute, Father, we could not thank you enough for all your goodness. But more important, our thankfulness ought to show in our daily lives. Forgive us when we do not let our thankfulness show in the way we choose to live. Guide us into a life style that will give evidence to the thankfulness we feel in our hearts. In Jesus' name we pray. Amen.

Hymns
"Amazing Grace! How Sweet the Sound"
"How Great Thou Art"
"Standing on the Promises"
" 'Tis So Sweet to Trust in Jesus"

PROPER 9
Sunday between July 3 and 9 inclusive

Gospel: Mark 6:1-6
Theme: Jesus rejected in Nazareth

Call to Worship
Pastor: God's love and redeeming grace is great enough to save the worst sinner.
People: We believe that. But we also know God's love can be rejected, and salvation does not happen.
Pastor: Jesus experienced that in Nazareth. They were without faith, and Jesus could not help them.
People: May Jesus find us firm in our faith so he can transform our lives by his saving grace.

Collect
Gracious Father, whose Son was rejected by those who saw only his humanity and not his divinity, making their salvation hopeless: Open our hearts to the healing ministry of our Savior, that he may save us from the power of sin and death. In his name we pray. Amen.

Prayer of Confession
How often you are in our presence, Father, and our indifference keeps us from receiving the miracle of your forgiving grace! We take you for granted, because we have heard about you all our life. Forgive us when we refuse to listen to your word, or to be touched by your love. Renew our faith in Christ, that we may be ready and willing to have him restore us to new life. In his name we pray. Amen.

Hymns
"Come, Ye That Love the Lord"
"Draw Thou My Soul, O Christ"
"Have Thine Own Way"
"My Faith Looks Up to Thee"

PROPER 9
Sunday between July 3 and 9 inclusive

Second Lesson: 2 Corinthians 12:1-10
Theme: In weakness we experience Christ's strength

Call to Worship
Leader: We each have our own weakness, but that does not need to hinder our discipleship.
People: We have felt inadequate, inferior, and quite worthless at times. And yet we know the joy of Christian discipleship.
Leader: If we could boast of our own strength, we would hinder Christ working through us, and little would be accomplished.
People: Our strength is in Christ who uses us in spite of our weaknesses. We are glad to give him the glory!

Collect
Eternal God, whose Son is the strength of your church, and who accomplishes much in spite of our human limitations: Make us alive and effective in our ministry, strengthened by the presence of Christ, that we may not hinder the growth of your church by our inabilities. We pray through Christ our Lord. Amen.

Prayer of Confession
There are so many things we cannot do well, Father, and we tend to give up. Sometimes we are proud of our abilities, and feel we have succeeded on our own strength. Forgive us when we have hurt the ministry of your church by not letting Christ be our strength. Take our inadequacies, and prove your power through a living vital church, committed to our Lord Jesus Christ, through whom we pray. Amen.

Hymns
"Christ is Made the Sure Foundation"
"God Is My Strong Salvation"
"Jesus My Strength, My Hope"
"The Church's One Foundation"

Nov 10

PROPER 9
Sunday between July 3 and 9 inclusive

First Lesson: 2 Samuel 7:1-17
Theme: God's providence

Call to Worship

Leader: In all of life, there is nothing so wonderful as God's providence.
People: God is so good. He guides, protects, provides, strengthens, loves, and forgives!
Leader: We could go on and on, and never exhaust all the wonderful things God does for us.
People: We give thanks to God for caring so much for us.

Collect

Almighty God, whose main concern is the welfare of your people: May our praise and thanksgiving be as unending as your daily blessings that go on without end from one generation to the next. It is through Christ that we give you our praise. Amen.

Prayer of Confession

Eternal God, you are forever caring for us as a father cares for his children! Forgive us when we take such love for granted without responding with praise and thanksgiving. Accept our offerings of praise now; and keep us ever mindful of your blessings, and vocal in our appreciation. In the name of Christ we pray. Amen.

Hymns

"God of Our Life"
"Now Thank We All Our God"
"Praise to the Lord, the Almighty"
"We Come unto Our Fathers' God"

PROPER 8
Sunday between June 26 and July 2 inclusive

Gospel: Mark 5:21-43
Theme: Miracles which illustrate salvation

Call to Worship

Leader: Sin appears to have power over us through the reality of death.
People: Death is real, but not final, because Christ our Savior has even greater power!
Leader: Christ is redemptive! All of us can experience the miracle of salvation and the miracle of life after death!
People: We know Christ is our Savior! We thank God for the faith he has placed within our hearts!

Collect

Gracious heavenly Father, who redeems our lives from the power of sin and death through your Son Jesus: Touch our lives with the healing of our souls; that we may be assured of our victory over sin and the grave to live victoriously with Christ our Redeemer, in whose name we pray. Amen.

Prayer of Confession

We want to be made whole, Father, assured that our sins are forgiven and our lives secure in your love. But sin makes us deny our devotion, and we feel unsure of our eternal destiny. Forgive us when we are insincere in our commitment, and sacrilegious with our lifestyles. Redeem us from the grip of sin; that we may be free to live a new life for you, made whole by the healing touch of Christ our Savior, through whom we pray. Amen.

Hymns

"Amazing Grace"
"Jesus, Thy Blood and Righteousness"
"O For a Thousand Tongues to Sing"
"Pass Me Not, O Gentle Savior"

PROPER 8
Sunday between June 26 and July 2 inclusive

Second Lesson: 2 Corinthians 8:7-15
Theme: Christian stewardship of money

Call to Worship
Pastor: We measure wealth in terms of money. But our greatest wealth is the salvation Christ gives to us.
People: We are wealthy, spiritually, because Christ was willing to make himself poor on our behalf.
Pastor: That is why material wealth is a sacred trust. We give for the sake of others as Christ gave for our sake.
People: May the love of Christ flow through his church as we take seriously the needs of others.

Collect
Benevolent Father, whose Son became poor that we might become rich: Move us with genuine compassion to give freely of our wealth, that your church may be effective in its ministry to lift others out of spiritual poverty. We pray through Christ our Redeemer. Amen.

Prayer of Confession
We are wealthy people, Father, who prefer to complain about our debts rather than rejoice in your benevolence. Forgive us for selfishness which makes us ask of you in our prayers, but say no to others with our contributions. Give us a desire to support your church financially, not because of church bills, but because of the great gift you have given in Christ Jesus our Savior, through whom we pray. Amen.

Hymns
"As Men of God Their First Fruits Brought"
"I Gave My Life for Thee"
"More Love to Thee"
"We Give Thee But Thine Own"

PROPER 8
Sunday between June 26 and July 2 inclusive

First Lesson: 2 Samuel 6:1-15
Theme: The Ark is brought to Jerusalem

Call to Worship
Pastor: When we come into the sanctuary, we feel the presence of God.
People: We know God is everywhere, but we feel especially close to him here.
Pastor: The altar helps us to sense the nearness of God, and undergrids our worship of him.
People: We know God is here, and offer ourselves in praise and devotion.

Collect
Eternal God, whose presence is always about us: Help us to make our hearts your altar; that we may live and serve in the awareness that you are in our midst. In our Savior's name we pray. Amen.

Prayer of Confession
We need your presence, Father, to guide, strengthen, and protect us. But sometimes we are afraid of your presence because of our unworthiness. Forgive us when we try to keep our distance, thinking we are safer. Come into our lives and bless us with your grace and power; and give us your peace. In the name of Christ, we pray. Amen.

Hymns
"I Need Thee Every Hour"
"Nearer My God to Thee"
"O For a Closer Walk with God"
"When the Storms of Life Are Raging"

PROPER 7
Sunday between June 19 and 25 inclusive
(If after Trinity Sunday)

Gospel: Mark 4:35-41
Theme: Jesus stills the storm

Call to Worship

Pastor: Life is not without its storms; but remember, our storms are not without our Savior!

People: We know fear, but we also know faith. And Christ has stood by us in our storms.

Pastor: Our Lord has power to bring peace to our troubled souls, if only we trust him to be the Lord he is.

People: We know who Jesus is, and trust him to overcome any fear which would destroy our faith.

Collect

Almighty God, whose Son is in command of life and stills the tempests which would trouble our souls: Increase our faith in his divine authority, that life may not toss us about at the mercy of our fears. In our Savior's name we pray. Amen.

Prayer of Confession

Our Father, we confess that fear has left its mark on each of us. We desire faith, and many times feel strong. But our mortal nature seems to have an overpowering force, and we become troubled for fear that life would destroy us. Forgive us when our faith does not reveal the presence of Christ who is able to calm our anxiety. Undergird us with confidence in our Lord's presence, that we may be defended against all tribulation. We pray through Christ our Lord. Amen.

Hymns

"Be Not Dismayed"
"Peace, Perfect Peace"
"Thou Hidden Source of Calm Repose"
"When the Storms of Life Are Raging"

PROPER 7
Sunday between June 19 and 25 inclusive
(If after Trinity Sunday)

Second Lesson: 2 Corinthians 5:18—6:2
Theme: We live for Christ who died for us

Call to Worship

Leader: Our sinful nature compels us to live selfishly without concern for others.
People: **But our love for Christ compels us to live not for ourselves, but for him.**
Leader: Amen! It is Christ who died for us, and was raised to life who now determines our lifestyle.
People: **We are glad to be Christians, and want our lives to show that we live for Christ.**

Collect

Gracious Father, whose Son died and was raised to life for our sake: Fill our hearts with committed love to him; that we may no longer live for ourselves, but for Christ our Savior, in whose name we pray. Amen.

Prayer of Confession

Life is a precious gift, Father, which you give to us. But we confess we become selfish with it, even with our knowledge of Christ's sacrifice on our behalf. Forgive us when we live to satisfy our desires, instead of living to please our Savior. Unite us with Christ, that we may experience a new creation of our total being. In his name we pray. Amen.

Hymns

"Have Thine Own Way, Lord"
"I Am Thine, O Lord"
"Just As I Am, Thine Own to Be"
"My Jesus, As Thou Wilt"

PROPER 7
Sunday between June 19 and 25 inclusive
(If after Trinity Sunday)

First Lesson: 2 Samuel 5:1-12
Theme: David's kingdom established by God

Call to Worship
Pastor: The strength of our nation lies in our devotion to God.
People: We cannot build a government that will survive if God's will is ignored.
Pastor: God's purpose for all nations is to serve in the best interest to all people.
People: May our nation be truly "under God" and fulfill his purpose in our world.

Collect
Almighty God, who is the chief architect for society: Inspire the nations of this land with a passion for human rights; that our world may become a community in which oppression is removed, and freedom is a universal blessing. In Christ's name we pray. Amen.

Prayer of Confession
We are proud of our nation, Father, and thank you for the privilege of being citizens. But our pride often causes us to leave you out of the picture. Forgive us when we reject your guidance in our national and international concerns. Help us to build a nation that sees the world as one family in which we share your concern and compassion with all people. We pray through Christ our Lord. Amen.

Hymns
"God of Our Fathers"
"My Country, 'Tis of Thee"
"O Beautiful for Spacious Skies"
"This Is My Song"

PROPER 6
Sunday between June 12 and 18 inclusive
(If after Trinity Sunday)
Gospel: Mark 4:26-34
Theme: Parables of the Kingdom

Call to Worship
Pastor: God has established his kingdom, and invites each of us to be a part of it.
People: We do not understand everything about the Kingdom of God, but we do know it is a blessing we can experience.
Pastor: God increases his Kingdom as persons respond to the work of his Spirit.
People: We pray for God's Spirit to find responsive hearts, that his Kingdom may advance throughout the earth.

Collect
Almighty God, who increases your Kingdom wherever hearts are responsive to the work of your Holy Spirit: Work in our midst, that the feeble attempts of your church may be multiplied into great advances for your Kingdom. We pray in Jesus' name. Amen.

Prayer of Confession
We are your church, O God, and we struggle to make your church great. How often we fail to recognize that your Kingdom will advance only when we commit our efforts to you rather than our own institution. Forgive us when we feel our labors are independent of what you are doing through your Holy Spirit. Guide us in the consecration of our efforts to support your Kingdom rather than struggle to build our organization. We pray through Christ our Lord. Amen.

Hymns
"Come, Thou Almighty King"
"Father Eternal, Ruler of Creation"
"Jesus Shall Reign"
"Lead On, O King Eternal"

25 Aug 85

PROPER 6
Sunday between June 12 and 18 inclusive
(If after Trinity Sunday)

Second Lesson: 2 Corinthians 5:6-10, 14-17
Theme: Encouraged by our faith

Call to Worship
Pastor: The Christian life is not a means of material gain, but a source of spiritual blessing.
People: We enjoy the physical life God gives, but our faith assures an even fuller life for those who are faithful to God.
Pastor: Faith gives us courage when fear would discourage us, for we know Christ is our source of strength.
People: Praise God for faith through which he grants us courage to be Christians!

Collect
Gracious Father, who encourages us to live by faith in your Son, our Savior: Increase our faith to be loyal disciples, that we may be strengthened against adversity and give a true witness to your love and power. We pray through Christ our Lord. Amen.

Prayer of Confession
We know the pain of discouragement, Father, because we put so much confidence in the happiness of this world. Forgive us when we lose sight of the spiritual world and lose courage to resist the influence of this world. Bless us with your presence as a means of strengthening our faith; that we may learn to live courageously, and please you with our discipleship. Hear us for Jesus' sake. Amen.

Hymns
"God of Grace and God of Glory"
"He Who Would Valiant Be"
"March On, O Soul, with Strength"
"O For a Faith that Will Not Shrink"

PROPER 6
Sunday between June 12 and 18 inclusive
(If after Trinity Sunday)

First Lesson: 2 Samuel 1:1, 17-27
Theme: David's lament over Saul and Jonathan

Call to Worship

Pastor: Grief is a part of our humanness we must live with.
People: It is a painful experience when we lose a loved one in death.
Pastor: Our grief is softened when we take it to the Lord, who gives the comfort of his Spirit.
People: We are thankful for the healing God gives to us in our grief when we share it with him.

Collect

Gracious Father, who knows the pain we suffer when a loved one dies: Send your Spirit to all who mourn; that they may find comfort for their sorrow; and be strengthed in their faith. We pray in the name of Christ our Lord. Amen.

Prayer of Confession

Father, we confess our weakness in accepting the death of our loved ones. Thank you for the hope you have given us through your risen Son. Forgive us when we are so grieved that we resist the comfort of your Spirit. When in sorrow, lift us by your Spirit to know you are sharing our pain with us. In our Savior's name, we pray. Amen.

Hymns

"Abide with Me"
"I Know Not What the Future Hath"
"On Jordan's Stormy Banks I Stand"
"Sing with All the Sons of Glory"

PROPER 5
Sunday between June 5 and 11 inclusive
(If after Trinity Sunday)

Gospel: Mark 3:20-35
Theme: Sin against the Holy Spirit

Call to Worship

Pastor: Holy is the Lord, Father Almighty, who made heaven and earth.

People: We give praise to God, our Creator, Redeemer, and Judge.

Pastor: The holiness of God is the source of our salvation from sin. To deny God's holiness is to be judged guilty of sin.

People: Our faith is in Christ Jesus who has demonstrated the power, love and authority of the holy God, our heavenly Father.

Collect

Heavenly Father, whose holiness is not to be challenged or denied: Convince us by your Holy Spirit of our sinfulness and your redemptive love, that we may not be judged guilty of denying your righteous authority over our lives. We pray through Christ our Redeemer. Amen.

Prayer of Confession

We believe your grace is great enough to remove the guilt of our sins, Father. Yet, in our careless way of living, we take lightly your holiness, and the authority you have to judge us. Forgive us if we have acted willfully or unwillfully in any way which suggests we do not acknowledge your holiness or authority. Cleanse us by the blood of Christ our Savior, and lead us in a life which gives glory and praise to you. In our Savior's name we pray. Amen.

Hymns

"Holy God, We Praise Thy Name"
"Holy, Holy, Holy! Lord God Almighty"
"Love Divine, All Loves Excelling"
"Take Time to Be Holy"

PROPER 5
Sunday between June 5 and 11 inclusive
(If after Trinity Sunday)

Second Lesson: 2 Corinthians 4:13 — 5:1
Theme: Live by faith

Call to Worship
Pastor [Leader]: Life brings us trouble and pain. But our faith convinces us of our eternal glory which is much greater than the trials of this temporary life.
People: **We live by faith, believing God blesses us with much more than what this world can give.**
Pastor [Leader]: Our physical life will end, but we know God will bless us with life that goes on forever!
People: **We do not fear the suffering of this life, because we look forward to eternal joy where there will be no pain or sorrow!**

Collect
Gracious Father, who has prepared for us the eternal blessings of love, joy, and peace: Encourage us in the difficulties of this life, that we may not lose sight of these unseen blessings which last forever. We pray through Christ our Lord. Amen.

Prayer of Confession
Life hurts us many times, Father, and we feel defeated. We look only at our present situation, and sometimes it overwhelms us. Forgive us when our faith is so weak that we fail to see the real life which you are offering to us. Give us a vision of the unseen reality of an eternal joy where we are forever at home in the security of your love. In our Savior's name we pray. Amen.

Hymns
"Be Thou My Vision"
"O Gracious Father of Mankind"
"O Holy Savior, Friend Unseen"
"Open My Eyes, That I May See"

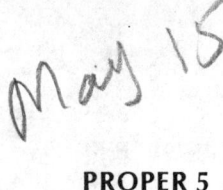

PROPER 5
Sunday between June 5 and 11 inclusive
(If after Trinity Sunday)

First Lesson: 1 Samuel 16:14-23
Theme: The peace of God

Call to Worship
Pastor: Life can be quite a battle field with all its struggles and conflicts!
People: There are many times when we need to be able to get in touch with God, and find his peace to calm our souls.
Pastor: God's peace is always available to us for whatever circumstances life may bring.
People: May God's Spirit rest upon us with the blessing of his peace throughout our days.

Collect
Heavenly Father, who desires to bring peace to our troubled souls: Come to us through your Spirit, and bring calm to our distress; that we may enjoy the life you want us to live. In the name of Christ we pray. Amen.

Prayer of Confession
We are too familiar with distress, Father, from all the responsibility and frustration we have. But we know we do not need to be overcome with our distress. Forgive us when we make life a struggle, instead of living victoriously in the blessing of your peace. Give us that victory now, as we yield ourselves to you. We pray in Jesus' name. Amen.

Hymns
"Be Not Dismayed"
"Come, Ye Disconsolate"
"Peace, Perfect Peace"
"When the Storms of Life are Raging"

PROPER 4
Sunday between May 29 and June 4 inclusive
(If after Trinity Sunday)

Gospel: Mark 2:23 — 3:6
Theme: The Sabbath, a symbol of salvation

Call to Worship
Leader: This is the Lord's Day, a day to worship God in thanksgiving for our salvation.
People: We praise God for the victory over sin which he gives through his Son, Jesus Christ!
Leader: We are freed from the bondage of sin; and this day is a public witness of how God has saved us.
People: May this day be a weekly symbol to our world that God has made us free. We rejoice in him!

Collect
Most holy Father, who has come in our midst to save us, and has set this day aside as a symbol of salvation to our society: Grant that we may live this one day in such a way as to give you honor and glory for our salvation in Jesus Christ, through whom we pray. Amen.

Prayer of Confession
We recall, Father, how we used to dread Sunday because of all the restrictions. Yet in our present freedom from those restrictions we feel we have also lost the purpose for calling this your day. Forgive us when we fail to let this first day of the week be a symbol of the salvation you have given through your Son. Direct us in our activities, that we may not misrepresent the salvation of which this day speaks. We pray through Christ our Lord. Amen.

Hymns
"Come, Let Us Tune Our Loftiest Song"
"Jesus, We Want to Meet"
"O Day of Rest and Gladness"
"Safely Through Another Week"

PROPER 4
Sunday between May 29 and June 4 inclusive
(If after Trinity Sunday)

Second Lesson: 2 Corinthians 4:5-12
Theme: Our weakness demonstrates God's power

Call to Worship
Pastor: The church is people who are mortal, and therefore weak compared to the mighty power of God.
People: Our weakness is often revealed when we struggle with the problems of our world.
Pastor: But our weakness also demonstrates that it is God's power which makes us, who are weak, victorious!
People: We commit ourselves to be instruments of God, that our weakness may reveal true victory in Jesus Christ.

Collect
Almighty God, who uses the weakness of our mortal nature to demonstrate your redemptive power: Convince us that, defeated as we sometimes feel, our weakness reveals your greatness; so that in spite of personal limitations and failures, you may gain a great victory over the power of sin. In our Savior's name we pray. Amen.

Prayer of Confession
We aim for greatness in the church, Father, even though we must confess we are weak against the force of evil. And that goal deceives our faith. Forgive us when we interpret apparent defeat as a poor witness to your mighty presence in our world. Help us to give ourselves to you, in trouble or adversity, confident that such situations will reveal your power and love. We pray through Christ our Lord. Amen.

Hymns
"Am I a Soldier of the Cross"
"Fight the Good Fight"
"God Is My Strong Salvation"
"He Who Would Valiant Be"

PROPER 4
Sunday between May 29 and June 4 inclusive
(If after Trinity Sunday)

First Lesson: 1 Samuel 16:1-13
Theme: David selected to succeed Saul

Call to Worship

Leader: It is a wonderful thing to be chosen by God for his service.
People: When God calls, it is a privilege to give ourselves on his behalf.
Leader: God chooses us, not because of our importance, but because of his need.
People: May we always see our service in the church as a calling of God; and be ready to serve as he demands.

Collect

Heavenly Father, who calls us into your service: Keep us mindful of who we are, what we are to do, and why we are to do it; that we may live a life of service on your behalf. In our Savior's name we pray. Amen.

Prayer of Confession

We are busy people, Father, and have good reasons for not doing more in the church than what we are doing. When we do work, our motivation is usually less than a divine call. Forgive us when we have not acted as servants on your behalf; and have seen our work as an unrewarding end in itself. Choose us as you see fit, and inspire us to do our best for your honor and glory. In Jesus' name we pray. Amen.

Hymns

"Forth in Thy Name"
"Lord, Speak to Me"
"O Jesus, I Have Promised"
"The Voice of God Is Calling"

FIRST SUNDAY AFTER PENTECOST
(Trinity Sunday)

Gospel: John 3:1-17
Theme: Born of the Spirit

Call to Worship
Pastor: Because of parents, we have life. Because of God, we have new life.
People: We are born again when God breathes his Spirit upon us, as though it were the beginning of a new life.
Pastor: Our conversion to the Christian faith is like that. We live a new life, led by God's Spirit.
People: May the Spirit of God breathe new life into our souls, that we may enter God's kingdom.

Collect
O God, our loving Father, who breathes new life into our souls by the gift of your Holy Spirit: Grant us your Spirit; that we may be born anew to live in the joy of salvation through Christ our Redeemer, in whose name we pray. Amen.

Prayer of Confession
We live from one day to the next, Father; but many times we feel we are existing rather than living. Our natural inclination to sin imprisons us in our physical world, preventing us from being born of the Spirit. Forgive us for narrowing life to the world of flesh and its desires. Open our hearts to the gift of your Spirit, that we may come alive with the joy of salvation. In our Savior's name we pray. Amen.

Hymns
"Breathe On Me, Breath of God"
"Father, I Stretch My Hands to Thee"
"Holy Ghost, Dispel Our Sadness"
"Holy Spirit, Truth Divine"

FIRST SUNDAY AFTER PENTECOST
(Trinity Sunday)

Second Lesson: Romans 8:12-17
Theme: Led by God's Spirit

Call to Worship

Pastor: We become God's children when we let his Spirit lead us.
People: Our sinful nature is strong, but God is our Father and defends us against sin by his Spirit.
Pastor: As God's Children we are assured that we shall possess eternal life which God gives through his Son, Jesus.
People: We trust God to lead us in a life of victory over sin and death.

Collect

Eternal God, who enables us by your Spirit to become your children: Inspire us to put to death our sinful desires; that we may call you our Father, and receive the blessing kept for those who are your children. We pray through Christ our Lord. Amen.

Prayer of Confession

Gracious Father, we are your children because you have created us. But we deny your fatherhood by our sinful behavior. We feel your Spirit directing us, and we turn the other way. We call you our Father, not because we live as your children, but because we want what you have to offer. Forgive us for our waywardness which brings us to you for selfish reasons only. Fill us with your Spirit, that our lives may proclaim you as our Father because of our love and loyalty. In our Savior's name we pray. Amen.

Hymns

"Be Thou My Vision"
"Come, Holy Spirit, Heavenly Dove"
"Lead Us, O Father"
"Spirit of God, Descend upon My Heart"

FIRST SUNDAY AFTER PENTECOST
(Trinity Sunday)

First Lesson: Isaiah 6:1-8
Theme: God's call to service

Call to Worship
Pastor: Holy, holy, holy is the Lord, God almighty!
People: The whole earth is full of his glory.
Pastor: Yet we have dared to come into his presence with praise and confession, to be commissioned in his service.
People: Here we are for God to use us as he sees fit.

Collect
Holy God, our Father, who has called us into your presence to share our adoration and devotion: Grant us your Spirit, undergirding us, in whatever you call us to do; that we may not fail in our service of Christ, your Son, in whose name we pray. Amen.

Prayer of Confession
How often we have been here, Father, and have taken your presence for granted. Yet we did not hear your call to service, nor did we expect it. Forgive us when we have concluded our worship services instead of going out to begin our services. Keep us mindful of your holy presence in all we do; that life itself may be our worship of you. In our Savior's name we pray. Amen.

Hymns
"Forth in Thy Name"
"God of Grace and God of Glory"
"Holy, Holy, Holy"
"I Love to Tell the Story"

THE DAY OF PENTECOST

Gospel: John 15:26-27; 16:4b-15
Theme: Jesus promises the Spirit of Truth

Call to Worship

Pastor: Jesus promised that God would reveal his truth through the Holy Spirit.
People: We do not know everything about God, but we do know the Holy Spirit inspires us with a truth which convicts us of sin.
Pastor: The law is limited in what it can reveal as right and wrong. But we all know the Holy Spirit convicts us of truth which the law cannot express.
People: We trust God to lead us by his Spirit in a life which reveals the way of truth.

Collect

Heavenly Father, whose nature and will is perfect truth; and who imparts that truth to us through the Holy Spirit: Inspire us with pure intentions and desires, that we may give an honest witness to the life which you desire all people to live. In our Savior's name we pray. Amen.

Prayer of Confession

We are people who are prone to sin, Father, but we defend ourselves by trying to make our sins look right, rather than confessing we are wrong. Forgive us for avoiding the conviction of our sins which you reveal through the Holy Spirit. Guide us in the true way to live; that we may benefit by the redeeming love of Christ our Savior, in whose name we pray. Amen.

Hymns

"Breathe on Me, Breath of God"
"God of All Power and Truth and Grace"
"Holy Spirit, Truth Divine"
"Spirit of Faith, Come Down"

THE DAY OF PENTECOST

Second Lesson: Acts 2:1-21 (or Romans 8:22-27)
Theme: The descent of the Holy Spirit at Pentecost

Call to Worship

Pastor: The church is a spiritual fellowship through which the risen Christ communicates his saving grace.

People: We are born of the Spirit, not by our own doing, but by the power and love of God.

Pastor: His Spirit is the source of our being, and the means by which we are able to share the gospel of Jesus Christ.

People: We pray that we may be receptive to the guidance of the Holy Spirit, that our witness may communicate the Savior's love to our world.

Collect

Almighty God, who has inspired your church in each generation through the gift of your Holy Spirit: Grant us the power to share the good news of Christ effectively; that those who hear may know what you have done through Jesus our Lord, in whose name we pray. Amen.

Prayer of Confession

We are your church, O God, but we fear we have made it more an organization than a spiritual force to bring our world into reconciliation with you. Forgive us when we open our lives to your love and close our hearts to the ministry for which your Holy Spirit would equip us. Break through the barriers our human nature creates in your church, and fill us with power and love to share the salvation our Lord has provided. In his name we pray. Amen.

Hymns

"Come, Holy Spirit, Heavenly Dove"
"Holy Ghost, Dispel Our Sadness"
"Spirit Divine, Attend Our Prayers"
"Spirit of God, Descend upon My Heart"

THE DAY OF PENTECOST

First Lesson: Ezekiel 37:1-14
Theme: The hope of restored life

Call to Worship

Pastor: Today is a celebration of new life.
People: We celebrate the life God's Spirit has breathed into the church throughout its history.
Pastor: God's Spirit has also breathed new life into our souls throughout our personal history.
People: We celebrate life, thanking God for the breath of his Spirit that makes living worthwhile.

Collect

Gracious Father, who restores life to your people through the breath of your Spirit: Breathe upon your church today; that we may come alive with all our energies to serve as living disciples of your Son, our Savior, through whom we pray. Amen.

Prayer of Confession

Father, we often become discouraged with the lack of influence the church has in our world. We wonder if our task is greater than our abilities. But then we remember the promise and power of your Spirit and realize we are not alone in our mission. Forgive us for our neglect of your Spirit when we work so hard without your guidance. Revive your church with new life to be the body of Christ in today's world. In his name we pray. Amen.

Hymns

"Christ Is Made the Sure Foundation"
"God of Grace and God of Glory"
"O God, Our Help in Ages Past"
"Spirit of Life in This New Dawn"

SEVENTH SUNDAY OF EASTER

Gospel: John 17:11b-19
Theme: Jesus' prayer for his disciples

Call to Worship

Pastor: Jesus consecrated himself to his redemptive act on the cross, that we might consecrate our lives to God.

People: We feel God helping us live the Christian life in a world of temptation.

Pastor: When Jesus consecrated himself, he asked God to undergird his followers with strength and loyalty.

People: We thank God for his help, and dedicate ourselves to faithfulness.

Collect

Almighty God, who keeps your children safe from the power of evil through the sacrifice of your only Son: Keep us loyal to our Savior, Jesus Christ; that we may be consecrated to a life of purity and righteousness, filled with the joy of those who belong to you. We pray in Jesus' name. Amen.

Prayer of Confession

We are willing Christians, Father, when it comes to taking the name of Christ. But we find many excuses when it comes to living a consecrated life. Forgive us when we avoid the dedication for which Christ prayed and died. Protect us from the temptation of insincere faith and uncommitted living. Take hold of our beings, and make us wholly yours, that we may be dedicated living witnesses of our Savior Jesus Christ, in whose name we pray. Amen.

Hymns

"Draw Thou My Soul, O Christ"
"Make Me a Captive, Lord"
"More Love to Thee, O Christ"
"Take My Life, and Let It Be Consecrated"

SEVENTH SUNDAY OF EASTER

Second Lesson: 1 John 5:9-13
Theme: Jesus is our source of life

Call to Worship
Pastor: We have gathered for worship. Let us proclaim our faith in Christ.
People: We believe Jesus is the Son of God, who died that we might be forgiven to live a new life with God!
Pastor: Such faith brings us in union with God our Father to experience life at its best.
People: Our life is in Christ. May we so live that others, too, may believe in the Son of God.

Collect
Wonderful God, our Father, who dwells in the hearts of those who believe in Jesus, your Son, blessing us with new life: Keep us ever faithful to your son; that we may enjoy your gift of life, not only now, but in eternity. In our Savior's name we pray. Amen.

Prayer of Confession
We are your church, O God, living examples of your Son, our Savior. But sometimes we are satisfied with only our knowledge of Christ instead of our experience. Forgive us for knowledge we have received that we have not put into practice in our lives. Help us to receive your Son both into our minds and in our hearts; that we may have the life only he can give. In his name we pray. Amen.

Hymns
"Father, I Stretch My Hands to Thee"
"Jesus Is All the World to Me"
"Take My Life, and Let It Be Consecrated"
"Thou Art the Way: To Thee Alone"

SEVENTH SUNDAY OF EASTER

First Lesson: Acts 1:15-17, 21-26
Theme: Matthias replaces Judas

Call to Worship

Pastor: Hear the invitation: Come and be a disciple of the risen Lord!

People: We are unworthy because of sin. But we are eligible, because we know our Lord's redemption.

Pastor: We become effective disciples when we live in commitment to Christ and in fellowship with those who serve him.

People: We feel called to serve our Lord, and pray that we may be faithful to our calling.

Collect

Eternal God, who is constantly calling persons into Christian discipleship as witnesses of our risen Lord: Inspire us to be faithful in our devotion to Christ; that our discipleship may give a faithful witness of salvation in Jesus, our Savior, through whom we pray. Amen.

Prayer of Confession

We consider ourselves to be Christian disciples, Father; but we feel it is more by our choice, than our being called into service. So when we do not choose as strongly to serve Christ, we do not feel we have neglected a special call. Forgive us when we are undependable in our discipleship and sporadic in our service. Convict us of apathy, and convince us of faithfulness; that we may be firmly established as disciples of Christ, in whose name we pray. Amen.

Hymns

"A Charge to Keep I Have"
"Jesus Calls Us O'er the Tumult"
"O Jesus, I Have Promised"
"O Master, Let Me Walk with Thee"

ASCENSION DAY
(Or the Sunday Nearest)

Gospel: Mark 16:9-16, 19-20 (or Luke 24:46-53)
Theme: The great commission

Call to Worship
Pastor: We are sent people, because our Lord's last words were a charge to preach the gospel to all mankind.
People: We have a message of salvation for all who will believe and be baptized.
Pastor: The body of believers is a powerful witness to God's redeeming love in Christ.
People: May all we do as Christ's church be done in Jesus' name, giving honor and glory to him.

Collect
Father in heaven, whose Son continues to reach mankind today through his body of believers: Make us effective witnesses on his behalf, that many may believe and be baptized into salvation. In our Savior's name we pray. Amen.

Prayer of Confession
We believe in spreading your good news, Father, so that all may hear, and be saved. But we support a few in their witnessing, rather than be witnesses ourselves. Forgive us when you have depended on our personal witness to win someone else, and we have failed. Give us the desire to let our lives be a means of interpreting the gospel to others; that we may not prevent anyone from believing in Christ, through whom we pray. Amen.

Hymns
"Christ for the World We Sing"
"Go Make of All Disciples"
"O Zion, Haste"
"We've A Story to Tell to the Nations"

ASCENSION DAY
(Or the Sunday Nearest)

Second Lesson: Ephesians 1:15-23
Theme: The exalted Christ

Call to Worship

Pastor: Christ our Lord has been exalted by God his Father, and rules with supreme authority.

People: We give Christ the highest praise, for worthy indeed is he who brought salvation!

Pastor: Christ has all authority over the church which continues to fulfill his mission of salvation.

People: How very great is the wonderful work Christ performs through his church!

Collect

Eternal God, whose exalted Son is the supreme ruler of our lives, and head of the church: Accept our humble devotion to serve him as his church, that your power may transform our commitment into a mighty force bringing your salvation to our world. In our Savior's name we pray. Amen.

Prayer of Confession

With great power, O God, you have given us your Son as our Savior. You raised him from death, and have exalted him with the highest honor. With that same power, you minister to our world through the church, the body of Christ. Forgive us, Father, when we become so indifferent to what it means to be the church, ministering in the name of our Savior. Strengthen us by your Spirit, to become the church which demonstrates a living Lord with power to redeem. In his name we pray. Amen.

Hymns

"All Praise to Thee, for Thou, O King Divine"
"Majestic Sweetness Sits Enthroned"
"The Church's One Foundation"
"The Head That Once Was Crowned"

ASCENSION DAY
(Or the Sunday Nearest)

First Lesson: Acts 1:1-11
Theme: The ascension of Jesus

Call to Worship

Pastor: Lift up your hearts in praise for our Savior whom God lifted into heaven!

People: We praise Jesus, our exalted Savior who is at the right hand of God the Father!

Pastor: Jesus has not left us, because he lives in our hearts; and we are witnesses of the new life he brings.

People: Glory be to Christ, God's Word made flesh, who manifests God's love to us!

Collect

Almighty God, whose Son ascended into heaven after his earthly life, instructing his disciples to be his witnesses: Inspire us with your Holy Spirit, that we may be filled with power to witness to the new life our Lord gives. In his name we pray. Amen.

Prayer of Confession

Father, we know you have exalted Christ in the highest heaven, with glory beyond anything we can comprehend. But we confess we have not exalted Christ within our own hearts. Forgive us when we take control of our lives instead of letting Christ be our authority. Give us the surrender which will let Christ lead us in a new life, enabling us to be faithful witnesses to the saved life which our Lord makes available to all persons. In his name we pray. Amen.

Hymns

"All Hail the Power of Jesus' Name"
"Crown Him with Many Crowns"
"Look, Ye Saints! The Sight Is Glorious"
"O For a Thousand Tongues to Sing"

SIXTH SUNDAY OF EASTER

Gospel: John 15:9-17
Theme: The ministry of love

Call to Worship

Pastor: We worship our Savior, Jesus Christ, who loves us even as God loved him.
People: Jesus was obedient to his Father, and remained in his love.
Pastor: Jesus challenges us to remain in his love by obeying his teachings.
People: Jesus has taught us to love one another as he has loved us. May God help us bear that kind of fruit in our lives.

Collect

Gracious Father, whose Son loved you enough to love us in our sin: Give us hearts capable of loving and being loved; that we may be obedient to the command of our Savior, Jesus Christ, in whose name we pray. Amen.

Prayer of Confession

We come in confession of our disobedience to our Lord's command to love one another, Father. We choose friends; but these are few, because we are not able to love as we are loved by our Savior. Forgive us for hindering the growth of your church and the joy of our friendship by restricting our love. Recreate us to be self-giving persons who are able to love; that we may become true friends of Christ, and true friends of all your children. In our Savior's name we pray. Amen.

Hymns

"At Length There Dawns the Glorious Day"
"Eternal Son, Eternal Love"
"Jesus, United by Thy Grace"
"O Brother Man, Fold to Thy Heart"

SIXTH SUNDAY OF EASTER

Second Lesson: 1 John 5:1-6
Theme: Victory over the world

Call to Worship
Pastor: Jesus is the Son of God. Believe that, and you are a child of God!
People: We do believe Jesus is God's Son. And we believe he is our Lord and Savior.
Pastor: Faith like that gives us victory over sin and death. Our Lord's triumph becomes ours!
People: We rejoice in our victory which Christ, our risen Lord, shares with us!

Collect
Almighty God, who enables us to overcome the evil of this world by faith in your Son, Jesus: Feed our faith daily by the inspiration of our risen Lord, that we may win a victory over all sin with which our world may tempt us. We pray through Christ our Lord. Amen.

Prayer of Confession
We continue to rejoice in Christ's victory over death, our Father. But we do not feel as victorious as those who believe in him ought to feel. Forgive us when we fail to grow in faith, not trusting in the power you provide through Christ to defeat the threat of sin. Give us the joy of victory by renewed faith in your Son, Jesus, who rose from the grave to give us a triumphant life. In his name we pray. Amen.

Hymns
"Be Thou My Vision"
"Fight the Good Fight"
"I Know Not Why God's Wondrous Grace"
"Soldiers of Christ, Arise"

SIXTH SUNDAY OF EASTER

First Lesson: Acts 11:19-30
Theme: The Gentile mission

Call to Worship
Pastor: The church is the body of Christ, made up of all persons who serve Jesus as Lord and Savior.
People: All national and geographical differences are overcome by God's gift of his Spirit.
Pastor: The Holy Spirit refreshes the lives of all who will repent, and put their trust in Jesus Christ.
People: We praise God for giving his love to all persons through his Son, Jesus, Savior of the world!

Collect
Heavenly Father, who has included all persons in your invitation to new life through your Son, Jesus: Increase our love which we express through Christian fellowship and witness, that your church may effectively share the Gospel with all persons. In our Savior's name we pray. Amen.

Prayer of Confession
We profess to be mission minded, Father, and pray for the church world wide. But much of the love we share is confined to an offering envelope to help people we do not really care to know. Forgive us for prejudices which keep us from being a loving church which is truly united in Christ throughout the world. Give us your Spirit; and enable us to understand that same Spirit is given to all who are your children. Thus may we heal the fractures and divisions in your church, the living body of Christ, through whom we pray. Amen.

Hymns
"All Praise to Our Redeeming Lord"
"Blest Be the Tie that Binds"
"Christ for the World We Sing"
"We've A Story to Tell to the Nations"

FIFTH SUNDAY OF EASTER

Gospel: John 15:1-8
Theme: Jesus is the true vine

Call to Worship

Pastor: We come together from many different places; but we are a part of each other, because we all belong to Christ.
People: We are like many branches of one vine; and Christ is that vine, uniting us to himself.
Pastor: We are united to Christ so that he may work through us to bear fruit in his kingdom.
People: We pray that many persons will be brought into God's kingdom because of our relationship with Christ.

Collect

Almighty God, whose Son desires that we remain in union with him for the purpose of bearing fruit in your kingdom: Keep us faithful to our Lord and Savior, that our witness may influence others to accept Christ as their Savior. In his name we pray. Amen.

Prayer of Confession

Dear Father, we are followers of your Son, Jesus; but much of our following is often from a distance. And so our discipleship does not bear much fruit. Forgive us when we have been satisfied with appearing to be Christian, without bearing the fruit of Christian discipleship. Unite us to Christ in a strong bond of love and loyalty, that the fruit of our labors may bring glory to you. We pray through Christ our Lord. Amen.

Hymns

"Blest Be the Dear Uniting Love"
"Draw Thou My Soul, O Christ"
"Have Thine Own Way, Lord"
"I Need Thee Every Hour"

FIFTH SUNDAY OF EASTER

Second Lesson: 1 John 4:7-12
Theme: God is love, so love one another

Call to Worship
Pastor: If we are God's children, we will love one another, because God is love.
People: Love for one another is evidence that we know the love God gives to us.
Pastor: Divine love restores life. God's love gives us new life through his Son, Jesus.
People: Praise God for his love which gives us new life in Christ! May we follow his example in loving one another.

Collect
O loving Father, who loves us enough to give us redemption through your only Son, Jesus: Grant us new life in Christ, that we may give evidence to your great love by loving one another as you have loved us. We pray in our Savior's name. Amen.

Prayer of Confession
We talk about love quite freely, Father, and praise you for your love. But it is much easier to talk about love than it is to love those with whom we talk. Forgive us when we sound so loving in our discussions, and then live as if we do not know how to love. Help us to receive in our hearts the love you give through Jesus, that our lives may tell the story of your love. We pray through Christ our Lord. Amen.

Hymns
"Blest Be the Dear Uniting Love"
"Blest Be the Tie that Binds"
"God Is Love; His Mercy Brightens"
"What Wondrous Love Is This"

FIFTH SUNDAY OF EASTER

First Lesson: Acts 8:26-40
Theme: Strength through fellowship with believers

Call to Worship

Pastor: Greetings in the name of Christ to all who are called by his name!

People: May the peace of Christ be in our hearts as we share our faith with one another.

Pastor: We are one in Christ, united to give and receive mutual strength to each other's faith.

People: May the Holy Spirit keep us true in our devotion to Christ as we encourage one another in the Christian life.

Collect

Heavenly Father, who strengthens us in our faith through the fellowship of Christian friends: Bind us together in true love and appreciation for one another, that we may each contribute to a growing faith in all who join our fellowship. We pray through Christ our Lord. Amen.

Prayer of Confession

Forgive us, Father, when our faith has grown cold by our indifference to the fellowship of Christian friends. Our schedules are full, and we seem to cut out church activities first. Then, before we know it, we lose the zeal of a vital faith, and life itself loses its vitality. Give us a warm personality which makes us seek out the companionship of those who believe in Christ, that we may give as well as receive the human support which the community of believers needs. We pray in Jesus' name. Amen.

Hymns

"All Praise to Our Redeeming Lord"
"Blest Be the Dear Uniting Love"
"Blest Be the Tie that Binds"
"Jesus, United by Thy Grace"

FOURTH SUNDAY OF EASTER

Gospel: John 10:11-18
Theme: The Good Shepherd

Call to Worship
Pastor: We worship Jesus who, like a good shepherd, laid down his life for us.
People: We worship Jesus who, like a good shepherd, knows each of us personally.
Pastor: We worship Jesus who, like a good shepherd, loves others whom he would like to bring into his fold.
People: We worship Jesus, our Good Shepherd, and give ourselves in obedience to his will.

Collect
Compassionate Father, whose Son gave himself in a ministry of loving care and redeeming grace: Bring us into his fold; that we may feel the blessing of his life restoring us to wholeness and protecting us from being ravaged by sin. We pray in our Savior's name. Amen.

Prayer of Confession
We wander around in life, Father, and try to convince ourselves it is a wonderful adventure. But we are lost, and cannot find our way. Forgive us when we lay aside self-discipline, divine guidance, and common sense in an attempt to find ourselves. Draw us closer to Christ, that we may understand his guiding presence in our lives which will keep us in his care. In his name we pray. Amen.

Hymns
"All the Way, My Savior Leads Me"
"He Leadeth Me: O Blessed Thought"
"Savior, Like a Shepherd Lead Us"
"Shepherd of Eager Youth"

FOURTH SUNDAY OF EASTER

Second Lesson: 1 John 3:18-24
Theme: Life which demonstrates God's indwelling Spirit

Call to Worship
Pastor: The Christian faith is more than just feelings we have in our hearts.
People: The Christian faith is a way of life in which we live by the convictions we feel.
Pastor: Such life brings us in union with God in which he blesses us with his presence.
People: May the words we express in worship bear the fruit of a life lived in obedience to God.

Collect
O loving God our heavenly Father, who dwells in the hearts of those who live in obedience to your commands: Cause our faith to become our way of life; that we may enjoy the blessing of living in union with you through your Son Jesus Christ, in whose name we pray. Amen.

Prayer of Confession
Our lips are familiar with the words of religious ritual, Father, and we are able to make our faith sound devout. But the life we live is not always in harmony with the faith we profess. Forgive us when our faith is without works, and our belief is not demonstrated by obedience. Help us to live a life which is true to our faith, that we may experience a fellowship of love with one another, and with you. We pray through Christ our Lord. Amen.

Hymns
"O Come, and Dwell in Me"
"Spirit of Faith, Come Down"
"Truehearted, Wholehearted"
"When We Walk with the Lord"

FOURTH SUNDAY OF EASTER

First Lesson: Acts 4:8-12
Theme: Jesus is our only Savior

Call to Worship

Pastor: Let us join in a celebration of Christ our Savior who makes us whole!
People: Praise be to Jesus, who died on the cross, and arose from the grave to give us victory over sin!
Pastor: Jesus alone is our Savior, for no one else is able to give us atonement with God.
People: We commit our love and devotion to Jesus, who alone cleanses us from sin and gives us a new life.

Collect

Heavenly Father, who has given your Son, Jesus, as our only Savior to bring us into your presence as people made whole: Refine our faith of any impure confidences, that we may put our whole trust only in Jesus, and be delivered from our sin. In his name we pray. Amen.

Prayer of Confession

Jesus is Lord! We believe that, Father, but we live in an age that questions the unique position of Jesus. In our acceptance of people of other religions, we find ourselves questioning that basic article of our faith. Forgive us when we lose sight of what you have done for all persons through Jesus alone. Reestablish us in our faith; that we may know salvation is ours only because of your gift of Jesus, in whose name we pray. Amen.

Hymns

"All Hail the Power of Jesus' Name"
"All Praise to Thee, for Thou, O King Divine"
"At the Name of Jesus"
"Take the Name of Jesus with You"

THIRD SUNDAY OF EASTER

Gospel: Luke 24:35-48
Theme: Jesus appears to his disciples

Call to Worship
Pastor: The risen Christ appeared to his disciples with the assurance that the Scriptures had been fulfilled.
People: The purpose of his life, death, and resurrection was to share God's message of forgiveness.
Pastor: The risen Christ still commissions his followers to be his witnesses, calling all people to repentance.
People: We serve the risen Christ, and take up the call to repentance, that all may hear of God's forgiveness.

Collect
Almighty God, whose risen Son calls his followers to go forth as his witnesses: Use your church today to lead our world to repentance, that all may experience your forgiveness. We pray through Christ, our risen Lord. Amen.

Prayer of Confession
We never cease to be amazed, Father, with the resurrection of your Son. But we are more amazed at life after death than the purpose of his resurrection. Forgive us when our devotion to the glory of his resurrection hinders us in witnessing to your message of salvation. Use us to share the good news of your forgiveness, that we may encourage many to repent from their sins. In our Savior's name we pray. Amen.

Hymns
"O Master of the Waking World"
"We Believe in One True God"
"We've a Story to Tell to the Nations"
"Ye Servants of God"

THIRD SUNDAY OF EASTER

Second Lesson: 1 John 3:1-7
Theme: We are God's children

Call to Worship

Pastor: We are the children of God. Therefore let us worship him with sincere hearts.
People: We are God's children because he loves us; and we worship God, because we love him as our Father.
Pastor: As children of God, we are challenged to live like Jesus in witness of God's fatherhood.
People: May we worship God each day as we live in obedience to our heavenly Father.

Collect

Heavenly Father, who created us in your image, and then reclaimed us as your children by the mercy of your great love expressed in your Son, Jesus: Give us the desire to be like Jesus, that we may offer to you the purity of those who desire to be called your children. Hear us for Jesus' sake. Amen.

Prayer of Confession

Dear God, we call on you as our Father, expecting you to hear us and help us. That implies we consider ourselves to be your children, but our lives do not speak well of being your offspring. Forgive us when our independence convinces us we can live as we please and still claim all the privileges of being your children. Inspire us to follow the example of Jesus' life, that we may give honor and glory to you. We pray through Christ our Lord. Amen.

Hymns

"Come, Ye (We) That Love the Lord"
"I Want A Principle Within"
"I Would Be True"
"Take Time to Be Holy"